Science and Technology

Handheld Gadgets

Neil Morris

www.raintreepublishers.co.uk
Visit our website to find out more information about Raintree books.

To order:
☎ Phone 0845 6044371
▤ Fax +44 (0) 1865 312263
▣ Email myorders@raintreepublishers.co.uk

Customers from outside the UK please telephone +44 1865 312262

Raintree is an imprint of Capstone Global Library Limited, a company incorporated in England and Wales having its registered office at 7 Pilgrim Street, London, EC4V 6LB – Registered company number: 6695582

Edited by Andrew Farrow, Adam Miller, and Diyan Leake
Designed by Victoria Allen
Original illustrations © Capstone Global Library Ltd 2011
Illustrated by Oxford Designers and Illustrators
Picture research by Elizabeth Alexander
Originated by Capstone Global Library Ltd
Printed and bound in China by CTPS

ISBN 978 1 406 22844 1 (hardback)
15 14 13 12 11
10 9 8 7 6 5 4 3 2 1

British Library Cataloguing in Publication Data
Morris, Neil.
  Science and technology: handheld gadgets -- (Sci-hi)
  680-dc22
A full catalogue record for this book is available from the British Library.

Acknowledgements
The author and publishers are grateful to the following for permission to reproduce copyright material: Alamy pp. **4** bottom (© Ianni Dimitrov), **16** (© Stacy Walsh Rosenstock), **30** (© Ian Shaw), **33** (© Ojo Images Ltd), **39** (© 67photo), **40** (© Synthetic Alan King); Corbis pp. 12 (© J. L. Cereijido/epa), **27** (© HO/Reuters), **35** (© Tim Pannell), **37** (© Eddie Keogh/Reuters); © Corbis p. **20**; Getty Images pp. **8** (Barbara Sax/AFP), **11** (Jason Alden/Bloomberg), **14** (Sankei); gps.gov p. **22**; iStockphoto p. **34** (© Simon Podgorsek); Rex Features p. **38** (Matti Bjorkman); Science Photo Library p. **36** (Ian Hooton); Shutterstock , **contents page** top (© Peter Grosch), **contents page** bottom (© Eduardo Rivero), pp. **4** top (© sextoacto), **6** (© Eduard Stelmakh), **9** (© Theodore Scott), **10** (© Chris Baynham), **15** (© Dino O.), **17** (© DMSU), **18** (© Gemenacom), **19** (© Peter Grosch), **21** (© Pincasso), **25** (© Alberto Zornetta), **26** (© Phil Date), **28** (© Avava), **32** (© Eduardo Rivero), **all background and design features**; SSPL p. **24** (© Science Museum); Thoroughbred Ford/Ford p. **41**.

Main cover photograph of a smartphone, reproduced with permission of Getty Images (Bloomberg); inset cover photograph of a brain reproduced with permission of shutterstock (© Lukiyanova Natalia/frenta).

The publisher would like to thank literary consultant Nancy Harris and content consultant Suzy Gazlay for their assistance in the preparation of this book.

Every effort has been made to contact copyright holders of material reproduced in this book. Any omissions will be rectified in subsequent printings if notice is given to the publisher.

Contents

The whole world in your hands   4

Computers   6

Phones   12

E-waste   18

Navigation assistants   20

Global Positioning System   22

Calculators   24

Games   26

Audio   28

E-readers   30

Cameras   32

Scanners   36

Remote control   40

Keeping safe   42

Quick quiz   43

Glossary   44

Find out more   46

Index   48

Some words are shown in bold, **like this**. These words are explained in the glossary. You will find important information and definitions underlined, <u>like this</u>.

What is e-waste? Turn to page 19 to find out!

What do megapixels do? Find out on page 32!

The whole world in your hands

Gadgets are small devices that we find useful. In this book we will look at some gadgets that are small enough to hold in our hands. This makes them even more useful, because we can use them on the move.

Handheld gadgets are getting smaller and more powerful all the time. Look at mobile phones, for example. Modern **smartphones** are mobile phones that are tiny computers. They take photos and make videos. Many of them can communicate via the internet (see page 9) and do many other things, too.

Unplugged

Gadgets need to be totally **portable**. This means you can hold them in your hand and move about as much as you want. Most use batteries you can recharge (top up the power for). That's the difference between a desktop computer and a laptop, or between a landline phone and a mobile phone.

Smartphones can take photos and send them to other phones.

How electronic gadgets work

Electronic gadgets work with the help of small **components** (parts), such as **microchips** and **transistors**. These components control and direct tiny amounts of electricity. Scientists have gradually made them smaller, lighter, and more powerful. When we press a key or a button to write a text or take a photo, the electronic component turns our action into a stream of numbers. This is a kind of code. The gadget either stores the numbers or sends the code to another device. The new device receives the signal and turns the code back into the original text or photo.

Waves of energy

Electronic gadgets use various forms of energy (power) to communicate with each other. These rays of energy come originally from the Sun. The rays of energy are called **electromagnetic radiation**, which travels in waves (see the diagram on the right). Handheld gadgets use **radio waves** to communicate with each other.

E-GADGETS

We also use the word *electronic* to refer to anything which involves the use of a computer. This is what the "e-" stands for when we send email, or read an e-book on an e-reader.

*This diagram shows the range of electromagnetic waves. The low-**frequency** waves have the least energy and the high-frequency ones have the most.*

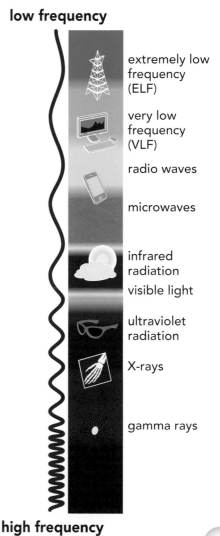

low frequency

extremely low frequency (ELF)

very low frequency (VLF)

radio waves

microwaves

infrared radiation

visible light

ultraviolet radiation

X-rays

gamma rays

high frequency

COMPUTERS

Home computers were introduced in the late 1970s. They were originally desktop machines. As use of the internet grew, people wanted to be able to move around with their personal computer. This led to portable versions with rechargeable batteries. The screen folded out from the keyboard, and eventually smaller versions had **touchscreens**.

Laptops

Laptops are small and light enough to sit on a user's lap. Smaller versions are often called notebooks. A laptop's battery recharges when it is plugged into a mains electricity socket. It can power the computer for several hours. As well as a display and a keyboard, a laptop has a **touchpad** that does the same job as a computer **mouse**. Laptops have become very popular in recent years. Many people use them instead of a desktop computer.

The battery and clear screen of a modern laptop mean that it can be used anywhere.

PERSONAL ORGANIZERS

Many people like to keep an up-to-date diary and address book in one place. Before computers became small enough to be portable, paper booklets were kept in leather wallets to form personal organizers. Other pieces of stationery could also be kept in the same place. These are still popular with some users, but electronic personal organizers, or **digital assistants**, have replaced most paper versions.

PDAs

A personal digital assistant (PDA) is sometimes called a palmtop computer. This is because it is small enough to be held in the palm of your hand. PDAs first appeared in the 1990s. They had the same features as earlier paper versions. They had a diary (or appointments calendar), an address book, and a program for creating the text (or words) of memos and other notes.

In recent PDA models, small keyboards have been replaced by touchscreens. PDA programs allow users to transfer data to another computer, for **backup** and security. Since 1993, smartphones have taken over from PDAs, because they do all of these things and more. <u>Developments in technology mean that new smaller gadgets can do much more than old larger ones.</u>

Tablet computers and the internet

Tablets (**tablet computers**) are small computers with a touchscreen. Apple Inc. launched its iPad in April 2010 in the United States. They sold 3 million iPads in 80 days. Wireless connection to the internet is vitally important. It allows users to browse the **World Wide Web** (see opposite), send and receive email, and play games using their tablet computer.

WHO DID THAT?
APPLE MAN

In 1974, 19-year-old Californian computer technician Steve Jobs began working on new programs for video games. In 1976 he founded a computer company called Apple with two colleagues. By 1981 the company had sales of $335 million (c. £210 million). By 2009 Apple's sales were more than 100 times greater than that and Steve Jobs was still its boss. He has invented or helped invent many things used in computing.

This tablet computer uses software to turn the screen into a musical keyboard.

What is the internet?

The internet is a huge network of computers. It links millions of computers and the network stretches around the world. No one owns the internet. A non-profit organization called the Internet Society watches over it. Individuals connect to the network via companies called **service providers**, who allow them to use the World Wide Web. The World Wide Web is a set of documents contained in pages and websites (groups of pages). These are connected by electronic words or pictures called **hyperlinks**. Computers use **software** called **browsers** to search and move around the Web.

BRIGHT IDEA: INVENTING THE WORLD WIDE WEB

British scientist Sir Timothy Berners-Lee invented the World Wide Web in 1990. He created the first website for CERN, a scientific organization in Switzerland. Over the next 20 years, the Web grew enormously. In 2008, Berners-Lee established the World Wide Web Foundation. The Foundation aims to expand the Web and keep it free to use and open to everyone. In 2010, experts worked out that the Web contained nearly 15 billion pages.

This is what a portable computer looked like in the 1980s, before the internet existed.

Wireless networks

Portable computers use a wireless network, sometimes called Wi-Fi, to connect to the internet. The network sends information along wires to a device called a **router**. The router turns the information into radio waves, and a computer within its range can pick up these signals. Each Wi-Fi area is called a **hotspot**. The number of free-to-use hotspots in libraries, stores, and cafés is increasing.

touchpad

The touchpad on this laptop can also be used to control the cursor (pointer) instead of a mouse.

FROM QWERTY TO MOUSEY

Some handheld computers have a keyboard with the traditional QWERTY layout. It is named after the order of the first six letters in the top row. This system was introduced to typewriters in 1872. The mouse is another common handheld gadget. This pointing device moves a **cursor** (pointer) around the screen and is used for inputting commands.

Touchscreen technology

Touchscreens are perfect for portable computers, because they do away with the separate keyboard. Instead, the traditional QWERTY layout appears on the screen. <u>One of the most common touchscreen technologies works by storing electricity. The stored electricity is harmless. It is called an electrical **charge**</u>.

When you touch the screen with your finger, some of the charge moves to you. Then there is less charge on the screen. The drop in charge is measured at each corner of the screen. This allows the computer to calculate the exact position of the touch.

The touchscreen layout of letters on this tablet is the same as on a physical keyboard.

VIRUSES

<u>A computer **virus** is a program that can spread from one device to another by making copies of itself</u>. Viruses can damage or destroy a computer's information. If a virus is attached to an email and sent to a computer, it can infect the computer when the **attachment** is opened. Many viruses can be found by special anti-virus software that allows you to destroy them before they damage your computer.

PHONES

Mobile phones are the most popular handheld gadgets of the 21st century. In 1990, when mobiles were still new, there were 12 million mobile phone users around the world. By 2010 there were about 4,600 million mobile phones in use. This was enough for one mobile for more than two-thirds of the world's population.

From walkie-talkies to mobiles

In 1943 a Canadian inventor called Donald Hings developed a phone that used radio waves. People could use it to have a two-way conversation. It became known as a **walkie-talkie**. Walkie-talkies were hugely successful.

A US telecommunications expert called Martin Cooper made the first public mobile phone call in New York in 1973. His phone weighed 1 kilogram (2.2 pounds). Modern mobiles weigh less than a tenth of that. It was another 10 years before the first commercial mobile service began. Early mobiles cost the equivalent of more than £4,700 today!

Martin Cooper holds up one of his early handsets. It came to be known as the "brick phone"!

Cells

Mobiles are telephones that use radio waves to send the signal. When you make a call, a device called a **receiver** picks up the radio signal from your phone. It sends the signal on to another receiver, and so on until it reaches a device called a **transmitter** near the person you are calling. The transmitter sends out signals to mobile phones. The receivers and transmitters are called **base stations**. Each station covers an area of about 26 square kilometres (10 square miles). This area is called a **cell**.

Your mobile phone uses a built-in **antenna**. This is a device that sends and receives radio signals. When you are near the edge of a base station's cell, your phone's signal strength gets weaker. In a remote area, you might have no signal at all.

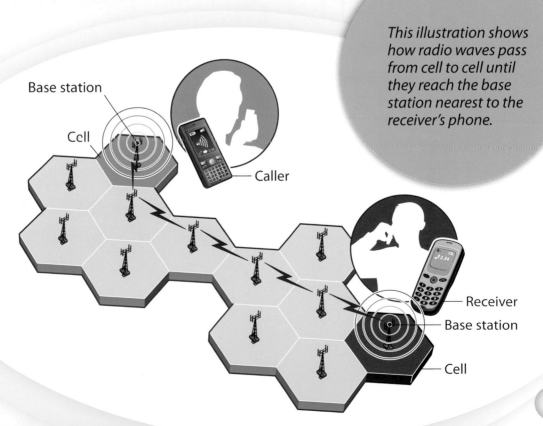

This illustration shows how radio waves pass from cell to cell until they reach the base station nearest to the receiver's phone.

Base station

Cell

Caller

Receiver

Base station

Cell

Smartphones

A smartphone does a lot more than make and take calls. It is really a handheld computer. You can use a smartphone to:

access the internet

send and receive phone calls and messages

send and receive email

find your position and the way to other places using information from **satellites** and maps

read e-books (electronic versions of printed books)

play audio and video files

keep a calendar and address book

do lots of other things using ready-made pieces of software that allow you to do things such as play games or draw cartoons

take photographs and make movies

Is mobile phone radiation harmful?

Small amounts of the radio waves from mobile phones go into the user's head. Some experts are worried about this. One study found that low-level radiation could cause sleep problems. But another found that it could protect against Alzheimer's disease (where sufferers lose their memory) in later life. Health authorities say there is no evidence of harm. However, they encourage people not to use their mobile too much. Long-term research will probably tell us much more about radiation and how much people are affected by mobile phone use.

What does a SIM card do?

SIM stands for Subscriber Identity Module. A SIM card is a portable memory chip. It has information about the personal details of a subscriber (the owner of the phone). The SIM card has two security passwords. There is a PIN (Personal Identification Number) which you put in to make the phone work. And there is a PUK (Personal Unblocking Key), which gets the SIM to work again if it has been locked. If you get your PIN wrong three times, your mobile will lock you out. The PUK will let you in again. The SIM card contains all your personal information, including your phone book. You can take it out and put it into another phone to make it work for you.

The gold-coloured memory chip of a SIM card sits in a piece of plastic. One corner of the plastic is cut off, so that it cannot be put in a phone the wrong way round.

STANDARD AND MICRO

Some phones use a new, smaller card called a micro-SIM. This can also be used in a phone designed for the bigger, standard SIM. You just need a plastic adapter card.

Mobile apps

Smartphones come with a number of **applications** (known as "apps") included. You can download more from the internet. Apple Inc has more than 200,000 apps for its iPhone. For students, there are a dictionary and thesaurus, measurement units converter, revision notes, school timetable manager, and world atlas. For cooks, there are recipes, shopping lists, and conversion tables for ingredients. Or you might want to play games, such as Charades, Harry Potter: Spells, or Scrabble.

The smartphone attached to this bicycle uses an app of a compass. This shows the direction that the cyclist is travelling.

SHORT MESSAGE SERVICE

Are you part of the "thumb generation"? That is, are you a texter, a sender of text messages, an SMS person? SMS stands for Short Message Service, which started in 1992 and has grown very fast since then. It has its own shorthand versions of words, such as *b4* for *before* and *CU* for *see you.*

Video, satellite, and cordless phones

Smartphones can use built-in cameras to send live video images across the world. This has done away with the need for separate **videophones**. Satellite phones are useful for journalists and emergency workers. They communicate with each other through satellites rather than base stations. There are no base stations in remote parts of the world but satellites can always be used. Cordless phones are simply handsets that connect by radio to base stations plugged into land lines.

Mobile phones can be very useful in an emergency. Climbers have even made calls from the top of the world's highest peak, Mount Everest.

SMS – SOS

On 18 August 2010, two British climbers were trapped in a storm 3,500 metres (11,480 feet) up the Italian Alps near Mont Blanc. Stuck on a ledge above a precipice (steep rock face), they could not move in the freezing conditions. They could not get through to emergency numbers on their mobiles. Both men's phone batteries were low, but they managed to text a friend in Shrewsbury, England – more than 1,000 kilometres away. They gave their location, the friend phoned the Italian emergency service, and a helicopter was able to lift them off the mountain.

E-WASTE

We all want the latest handheld gadgets. Models rarely last longer than a couple of years. Systems are upgraded and new designs become available. But what do we do with our old computers and phones? The last thing we want to do is add to a mountain of electronic waste.

Think of the waste if we just throw away our old mobile phones. If we really need a new phone, we should make sure the old one is reused or recycled.

What should we do?

Electronic devices contain **toxic** (poisonous) substances. They should never be thrown out with household rubbish. Many of the materials are recyclable. The device itself might be useful to someone else. So there are three main ways of dealing with the problem:

- return the product to the manufacturer
- take it to a professional waste disposal facility
- donate it to a charity.

We should also ask ourselves the question: do we really need the new model or can we update the old one?

What could manufacturers do?

The environmental organization Greenpeace International says:

"Our three demands are that companies should:
- Clean up their products by eliminating hazardous substances
- Take back and recycle their products responsibly once they become obsolete [no longer useable]
- Reduce the climate impacts of their operations and products."

Greenpeace also lists the greenest (or least environmentally damaging) companies every year. You can look this up if you want to check how green your own gadgets are (see page 46 for the web address).

This is just a small part of a large pile of e-waste. If we deal with old gadgets sensibly, we can fight pollution and help the planet.

STAYING PRIVATE

Whatever you decide to do with your old computer, phone, or other gadget, you should first remove all your personal details. This means wiping all discs, drives, SIM cards, or other memories or storage devices. Remember to remove all address books and similar lists.

19

NAVIGATION ASSISTANTS

In recent years motorists, cyclists, ramblers, and many others have come to depend on satellite navigation (often shortened to satnav). <u>Satnav acts like an electronic map to help people find their way</u>. Like many other electronic devices, satnav receivers have become smaller, more powerful, and therefore more useful. They all depend on the American Global Positioning System (GPS; see page 22). Russia, China, and the European Union are also working on new satellite systems.

GPS receivers

Personal navigation assistants (or PNAs) can be as small as a mobile phone. Their basic function is to give users their location, which is shown as a position of **latitude** and **longitude**. These measurements tell us positions on Earth's surface (see "Co-ordinates", opposite). But today they are much more user-friendly. They show maps, so that you can see exactly where you are.

These ramblers are using a GPS receiver to find their way. The device can show a map or give a list of instructions.

Co-ordinates

<u>Positions of latitude and longitude are called co-ordinates</u>. For example, the Empire State Building in New York is located at 40° 44′ 54.36″ N, 73° 59′ 08.36″ W. The first number is the latitude, given in degrees (°), minutes (′), and seconds (″) North. The second is the longitude in degrees West. The point at which these co-ordinates cross is the precise location. On the other side of the world, the Sydney Opera House is at 33° 51′ 25″ S, 151° 12′ 55″ E.

Use an atlas or a map to find out which famous landmarks are at:

a) 48° 85′ 83″ N, 2° 29′ 45″ E

b) 29° 58′ 45″ N, 31° 08′ 04″ E

c) 27° 10′ 27″ N, 78° 02′ 32″ E.

(Answers on page 46.)

Desert rescue

In January 2009, a Romanian tourist got lost for six days in the central Australian desert. Luckily he had a mobile phone and a handheld GPS device with him. He phoned his family in Romania and gave them his exact position from the GPS. They called relatives in Melbourne, who contacted the police. He was found and rescued, 22 kilometres (14 miles) from the settlement of Yulara, near the famous rock Uluru.

GLOBAL POSITIONING SYSTEM

The Global Positioning System (GPS) uses space satellites in orbit around Earth. The US Air Force operates the 30 or so satellites that are currently working. Twenty-four are enough to give complete coverage of the planet. A GPS receiver on Earth needs information from at least three satellites to work out its position.

The geometry of GPS

GPS works by geometry. That means, if you know how far you are from three other places, you can work out where you are. In GPS, the three other places are satellites in space.

The US space agency NASA launches rockets to carry satellites into space. The satellites send GPS information back to Earth.

DISTANCE AND THE SPEED OF LIGHT

Radio waves travel at the speed that light travels. That's about 300,000 kilometres (186,000 miles) per second! A GPS receiver works out where a transmitting satellite is by timing how long its radio signal took to arrive. Its computer does a lot of complicated maths!

How GPS works

Imagine you get lost in an unfamiliar country. First, you manage to discover that you are 30 kilometres from village A. That means you could be anywhere on this circle, because every point on the circle is 30 kilometres from the centre.

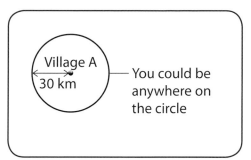

Then you learn that you are 50 kilometres from town B. This means you must be at one of the two points where the second circle meets the first. These are the only two spots that are 30 kilometres from A and 50 kilometres from B.

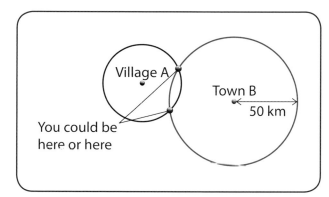

Thirdly, you find out that you are 75 kilometres from city C. Now you know exactly where you are. You are at the point where all three circles cross each other.

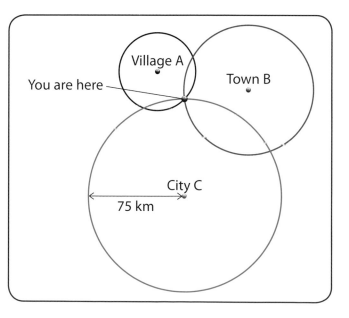

GPS works with spheres in three dimensions in space instead of circles in two dimensions on paper. This makes the calculations more complicated, but the idea is the same.

Calculators

Pocket calculators first became available in the 1970s. They changed many people's way of working. For the first time, people could do complex arithmetic quickly and accurately. They could also take their calculator around with them.

Early calculators were expensive. In 1974, an early model cost around £110, which is the equivalent of around £465 today. A similar model today would cost less than £6.25. Even so, it would be more powerful than the early calculators were.

WHO DID THAT?
ADDING AND SUBTRACTING

A French inventor called Louis Troncet developed a handheld mechanical calculator in 1889. His Arithmograph worked by moving rows of numbers with a metal pointer. Millions of these devices were sold.

In 1920 a German company started producing a machine called an Addiator. This did subtraction as well as addition. Later versions were still being produced in the 1980s.

More than 100,000 Addiators were sold in its first year.

What else can you "calculate"?

You can buy low-cost calculators that do lots of other things. Some calculators are also spellcheckers, crossword-puzzle solvers, and measurement converters. For example, they can quickly convert metres into feet or degrees Celsius into Fahrenheit. You can also buy handheld machines that include a dictionary, an encyclopaedia, a thesaurus, or a translator. One of these small machines can translate more than 200,000 words into six different languages.

A simple calculator like this can do all sorts of sums. It also has a memory, which makes it much easier to do big calculations.

solar panel

BRIGHT IDEA: SOLAR CELLS

You may have seen calculators with a solar panel at the top. The panel contains several **solar cells**. These are cells that power the device. The cells are **photovoltaic**. <u>Photovoltaic cells convert sunlight into electricity</u>. They are also used in solar chargers, which power up rechargeable batteries in other handheld devices.

GAMES

The first computer games appeared in the 1970s. They had special cases called **cartridges** with computer disks in them. But these could do nothing else. Manufacturers soon realized that people wanted to play video games on the move. This led to handheld games **consoles**, which were particularly popular with young people. At first the games were inserted on chunky cartridges. Today they use slim game cards. A console called Wii has a handheld remote control for playing games on a separate screen.

Games consoles are small devices that are easy to carry.

NDS and PSP

Scientists, engineers, and designers sometimes come up with different ideas on how to make things easy or interesting for the gadget user. This happened with games machines. The two best-selling portable consoles came from Japan in 2004. The Nintendo DS has a dual screen (DS). The upper screen is the game monitor, and the lower is a touchscreen for entering commands. Sony's PlayStation Portable (PSP) has a single viewing screen with playing buttons to right and left.

In this game, players try to help alien creatures and robots save the galaxy from evil forces.

Walkthroughs

"Walkthroughs" can teach you how to complete and win video games. They are put together by experienced game-players. Sometimes they are produced in the form of FAQs (Frequently Asked Questions), but for complicated games they take (or walk) you through the game. These walkthroughs are sometimes called cheats. It is up to you to decide whether it is cheating if you use them.

FROM MICROVISION TO GAME BOY

The first handheld game console was Microvision, produced in 1979. It had cartridges for different games, but not very many. It was not a success. It was followed 10 years later by a hugely successful console: the Game Boy. It was just right for its time, with the latest games and a good, simple design. Nearly 119 million Game Boys were sold. The follow-up Game Boy Advance has sold another 81 million.

AUDIO

Until the 1990s, portable music players depended on separate physical storage such as records, tape cassettes, or CDs (compact discs). This changed when the first digital audio players (DAPs) were created in 1997. <u>The new DAPs store, organize, and play audio (sound) files on **hard-disk drives** or memory cards</u>. They are often called MP3 players, after the name of the system they use for storing and playing sound.

Engineers developed different designs for different companies. They also developed various ways of getting music onto the players. In 2001, Apple Inc launched its iPod, which became the market leader in DAPs. In 2010 Apple said they had sold 250 million iPods.

These girls are sharing an MP3 player to enjoy music together. They are using earphones, but DAPs can also be put in a device called a dock and played through speakers.

PORTABLE MUSIC

The invention of the Sony Walkman in 1979 changed people's music-playing habits. This portable cassette player used headphones and was only slightly bigger than the cassette itself. It is said that the chairman of the Sony company wanted it developed so that he could listen to opera on long flights from Japan to the United States! Early models were called SoundAbout in the United States and Stowaway in the UK. But the name Walkman won through and it is still used.

Downloading and piracy

Modern technology makes it possible for us to do all sorts of new things with our gadgets. But it is important that we are responsible in what we do. For example, technology now allows us to download songs to our music player from online stores, such as iTunes or Amazon. But there are other websites which allow illegal downloads (called piracy).

Illegal downloads break **copyright** laws, which give creative artists the right to control their own work and earn money from it. The Recording Industry Association of America says: "Plain and simple: piracy is bad news. While the term is commonly used, 'piracy' doesn't even begin to describe what is taking place. When you go online and download songs without permission, you are stealing … Artists, songwriters, musicians, record-company employees, and others in the industry all lose money."

E-READERS

The electronic-book reading device (or e-reader) was developed in the 1990s. Most models today are about the size of a hardback book, so that you see and read one page at a time. They have buttons or a touchscreen for turning pages and other commands.

Overtaking print?

In July 2010, the bookseller Amazon announced that in the previous three months they had sold more e-books than printed hardback books. In one month, the company sold 180 e-books for every 100 hardbacks. That shows how much technology is changing the way we read books.

Manufacturers say that their e-readers have a "no glare, paper-like display".

Pros and cons

Arguments in favour of the e-reader:

- It takes up less space than printed books

- Its screen can be read in low light

- An e-book never goes out of print

- E-books are cheaper (although you have to buy the e-reader)

- E-books can be recovered if lost or damaged

- They can be downloaded and read immediately

- Printed books use three times more raw materials (paper and ink) to produce (without taking the e-reader into account).

Arguments against the e-reader:

- Individual e-books do not work on all readers

- Not all printed books are available as e-books (some authors will not give their permission to do this)*

- E-books do not have the physical feel of a book cover and paper

- E-books need batteries

- You have to buy an e-reader before you read a book, and it could be lost or stolen

- Customers cannot legally resell or lend their e-books to other readers

- E-readers are non-biodegradable, while paper is easily recycled.

HARRY POTTER

The author J. K. Rowling has not allowed her publisher to agree for her *Harry Potter* books to be published as e-books. In July 2010 her agent was reported as saying that she was considering changing her mind.

Cameras

The compact digital camera (or digicam) is the most popular camera today. By the turn of the 21st century, digital (computerized) technology was taking over from film photography. Since 1888, cameras had used chemicals to develop images from a thin strip of plastic (or film) and then make prints on paper. But digicams use an electronic process to capture images and save them on memory cards.

What are megapixels?

Digital cameras are often described in terms of how many megapixels they have. Pixels are tiny dots of light. Digital images are made up of millions of pixels. Megapixels measure resolution, which means the degree of detail visible in an image. The higher the number of megapixels, the more detail there is in an image.

More megapixels keep a picture sharp in close-up photography. This works if you enlarge a photograph, too, like this blow-up of the toucan's eye.

Point and shoot

Compact digicams are sometimes called "point-and-shoot" cameras. This is because the photographer does not need to adjust the camera in any way. It operates automatically. You just have to point it at your subject and press the button to take a photograph.

Live preview

The other advantage of digicams is "live preview". This means you can see exactly what you are photographing before you shoot, on an electronic display at the back of the camera. This is the same as the viewfinder on older cameras. You can also look at what you have just photographed instantly on the display. You can then decide to delete it or take another shot of the same subject. With film cameras, photographers had to wait to have the film developed to see their shots.

Point-and-shoot digicams take pictures without having to adjust settings on the camera.

Instant cameras

During the second half of the 20th century, the Polaroid instant camera was very successful. This was a film camera that developed photographs very quickly, so that the photographer had an instant print. Digicams have replaced Polaroids for most purposes, but the Polaroid company has brought out a new instant digital camera. This is a digicam with a built-in printer, so that you see your prints at once.

Early Polaroid cameras were bulky because they included the film packs for printing the photographs.

WHO DID THAT?
THE FIRST INSTANT CAMERA

Edwin Land (1909–91) was an American scientist who invented the first instant camera. It was called the Polaroid Land camera. He founded the Polaroid Corporation in 1937 and produced his first instant camera with black-and-white film 10 years later. In 1963, Land added instant colour film that developed within 50 seconds. The Polaroid was the best-known instant film camera.

Making movies

Earlier camera recorders (or camcorders) used video tape. But digital camcorders record on an internal memory called a hard-disk drive. They store hours of film material, which can easily be transferred to a computer or watched on a TV screen. Most compact digicams also shoot films as well as still images. They can be watched on the camera's monitor or transferred to a computer.

Compact digital camcorders are small and light. This makes them easy to use while on holiday.

YOU CAN BE A SPY!

Now you can buy a ballpoint pen which has a built-in digital video camera with microphone and includes a memory stick. The pen records for about 1 hour from one charge of the battery. It can store 15 hours of video and sound. The pen fits neatly into a jacket or shirt pocket. Advertisers say that the pen is perfect for undercover journalists and private investigators. What they really mean is it's perfect for spying. This gadget may be good fun, but some people would think that it invades their privacy.

SCANNERS

In the science fiction TV and film series *Star Trek*, characters use a handheld gadget called a tricorder. It scans data (information) and machinery, and is used for medical purposes, too. This must have seemed incredible to viewers when the series started in 1966.

Today, various gadgets, including smartphones, can achieve the same results as the fictional tricorder. Medical scanners are able to look inside a patient's body without doing any harm. Metal detectors use magnetic fields to help people search for ancient coins and other metal objects. Image scanners are used to reproduce pictures or documents.

Ultra-scanner

In 2010, an international healthcare company launched a handheld **ultrasound scanner**. This is a device that sends out sound waves. The sound waves bounce off internal body parts such as the heart. The scanner creates images from the waves that bounce back. The new flip-top scanner has a separate instrument which is held against the patient's body.

Ultrasound scanners are used regularly when pregnant women go for check-ups.

Scanning apps

There are many apps available to turn smartphones into medical scanners. More and more doctors are using them, but some have not yet been approved by the world's medical authorities. They want the phones to be tested more, so that they can be certain they are reliable.

In 2010, a researcher from University College London developed an app which turns a phone into a stethoscope for listening to a patient's breathing and heartbeat. There is even an app which asks patients to cough into their phone. It then tells them if they have flu, pneumonia, or another illness.

DETECTING GOLD

On 5 July 2009, Terry Herbert's metal detector helped him discover small objects beneath a ploughed field in central England. The objects were gold. Eventually more than 1,500 pieces were recovered. Experts said that they were about 1,400 years old. The sword fittings, crosses, and decorative items were cleaned and catalogued at the British Museum. They were valued at more than £3 million. Herbert and the owner of the farmland shared the reward between them.

These are just some of the gold objects found by Terry Herbert. The treasure was named the Staffordshire Hoard, after the English county where it was discovered.

Security wands

Security wands are used at airports and other places to scan passengers for metal objects, especially weapons. The wand is really just a small metal detector. A security officer waves the wand close to the passenger's body. The wand either bleeps or lights up to show that metal is nearby. Some police officers use silent versions which give a vibrating signal. This means that they are aware of the metal and can take action without alerting the person carrying the suspicious object.

This security wand is being used at the World Athletics Championships in Finland in 2005.

Barcode readers

Barcodes are patterns of vertical lines and numbers that identify an item and often its price. You will find one on the back of this book, showing its unique International Standard Book Number (ISBN). Handheld readers can decode the lines, which helps identify the book so that it is stored in the right place.

Barcode scanners

Barcodes also make it easy to count the amount of a particular book in stock. This can be useful in warehouses, bookshops, and libraries. People who work there can use a scanner to read the barcode, just as they do with goods in a supermarket.

Pointing the finger

Have you ever seen your own fingerprints? If you have, you'll know that the most amazing thing about fingerprints is that every finger is different. And everyone has a completely different set of fingerprints. Each one is unique. That makes fingerprints ideal for security devices. Fingerprint scanners can be separate or built into another gadget, such as a computer mouse. The scanner takes a digital image of your index finger. This can then be used to allow entry to a computer, certain programs, or even your front door. You put your finger on the reader and the reader scans it. If it matches the original, it allows you to carry on.
Your fingerprint is your password.

The police officer is scanning a person's fingerprint. The scan can be stored and used as evidence if fingerprints are found at a crime scene.

REMOTE CONTROL

The kind of TV remote control we use today was launched in the 1970s. It changed many people's viewing habits. Viewers liked being able to change channels without having to walk over to the TV set. It was not long before similar remote controls came in for hi-fi and other equipment.

Infrared signals

Most television remote controls work by **infrared** radiation. These rays have greater energy than radio waves (see page 5). When you point the device at your TV and press a button, it sends an infrared beam to a receiver in the TV. The receiver decodes the infrared information. It converts (changes) it into an electrical signal to change the TV settings.

The remote control is a familiar device in many homes now.

Into the future

The range and power of handheld gadgets have changed dramatically since 2000. Many of them, such as the latest smartphones, are really miniature computers with giant power. They allow us to keep in touch with each other via email, text message, and networking services. Many of the gadgets described in this book have helped create a revolution in communication. Will this continue in the future, with even newer ways of communicating? Or will future handheld gadgets have other uses that we are not even aware of yet?

MYSTERY CONTROL

"Most thrilling invention since radio itself! No wires. No plug-in. No cords of any kind! It's truly unbelievable! It's mystifying! That's why it's called Mystery Control!" This was how Philco advertised its wireless Mystery Control radio remote in 1939. It was the first handheld gadget of its kind. It was made of wood and quite chunky. You could change channels and alter volume with it, all from the comfort of your armchair. It used radio waves, not infrared like today's remote controls.

Other instruments we use today work like our handheld gadgets. This is a touchscreen dashboard in a car.

KEEPING SAFE

Gadgets can do amazing things, but things can go wrong. Here are some tips to help you keep your mobile phone and computer systems safe.

- Always back up your data on an external hard drive, CD, memory stick, or other device. Ask an adult for help with this if you need it.

- Always use passwords but avoid choosing obvious words or always using the same one.

- Install security software which protects against viruses (see page 11), spyware, and spam. Never open an email attachment that is in any way suspicious.

Identity theft

Your personal information is very useful to an identity thief, who can use your details by pretending to be you. Never give details to unauthorised people. If you suspect that someone is trying to get information – such as usernames, passwords, or other details from you – do not reply. Report it to a trusted authority. (This attempt to get your details is called phishing.)

- When checking emails: if in doubt, chuck it out.

- When online: if in doubt, log out.

Quick quiz

Try this quiz to see what you have learned about handheld gadgets. Then turn to page 46 for the answers.

1. Which of these waves and rays have the least energy?

a) X rays

b) microwaves

c) radio waves

d) infrared rays

2. What does SIM stand for?

a) security instant memory

b) safe install mouse

c) smartphone input modem

d) subscriber identity module

3. What should you NOT do with an old electronic gadget?

a) give it to a charity

b) throw it away

c) take it to a waste disposal unit

d) return it to the manufacturer

4. How fast do radio waves travel?

a) 300,000 kilometres per hour

b) 300,000 kilometres per minute

c) 300,000 kilometres per second

d) 300 kilometres per second

5. What kind of energy do photovoltaic cells use?

a) wind

b) nuclear

c) biomass

d) solar

6. What is image resolution measured in?

a) megapixels

b) megabytes

c) megabucks

d) megahertz

7. Who invented the instant camera?

a) George Eastman

b) Edwin Fuji

c) Edwin Land

d) Peter Polaroid

8. What is a security wand used for?

a) detecting banknotes

b) finding treasure

c) setting a password

d) detecting metal

Glossary

antenna device that receives and transmits radio signals

application (or **app**) computer program that performs a specific task

attachment file added to an email message

backup extra copies of something in case the original is lost

base station place in a cell that receives and sends mobile phone signals

browser computer program that helps you search for things on the World Wide Web

cartridge container holding computer disks, for example for playing computer games

cell area around a base station that receives and sends mobile-phone signals

charge quantity of electricity

component part of something, such as part of a gadget

console device with a set of controls – for example, for playing computer games

copyright legal right of creative artists to control their own work and earn money from it

cursor movable pointer on a computer screen

digital assistant electronic personal organizer with a diary, address book, and other features

electromagnetic to do with electricity and magnetism, especially in radiation from the Sun

frequency rate at which vibrations occur in a wave, such as a radio wave

hard-disk drive device that allows a computer or another electronic gadget to store information on a rigid disk

hotspot area where computers can use a wireless network to connect to the internet

hyperlink link from one part of a document to another that works by clicking on it or touching it

infrared referring to a kind of radiation that has more energy than radio waves but less than visible light

latitude imaginary line running around Earth, showing the distance north or south of the equator

longitude imaginary line running up and down the Earth from the North to the South Pole, showing the distance east or west of Greenwich, England

microchip small component that makes electronic gadgets work

mouse device that allows you to move a computer cursor, choose options, and give instructions

photovoltaic producing electricity from sunlight, as in a solar cell

portable designed to be easily carried around

radiation range of electrical and magnetic rays given off by the Sun, including radio waves

radio wave electromagnetic wave of energy that is useful for long-distance communication

receiver device that picks up radio signals

router device that connects individual computers to the internet

satellite object that orbits the Earth in space and can receive and send signals

service provider company that connects people and their computers to the internet

smartphone mobile phone that has functions that allow you to use it as a computer

software computer programs that give instructions to make a computer perform tasks

solar cell device that turns sunlight into electricity

tablet computer small computer with a touchscreen

touchpad small panel on a computer that acts like a mouse and allows you to move a cursor and choose options

touchscreen screen that shows options that you choose by touching them with your finger

toxic poisonous, very harmful

transistor small component that makes electronic gadgets work

transmitter device that sends radio signals

ultrasound scanner device that uses high-frequency sound waves to create images

videophone telephone that sends and receives pictures as well as sound

virus in computing, a program that can spread from one device to another and damage or destroy information

walkie-talkie portable two-way radio transmitter and receiver

World Wide Web vast set of documents contained in websites and pages on the internet

Find out more

Books

The Computer (Tales of Invention), Chris Oxlade (Raintree, 2010)

Digital Music (Culture in Action), Claire Throp (Raintree, 2010)

Gadgets and Inventions (From Fail to Win), Neil Morris (Raintree, 2010)

Social Networks and Blogs (Mastering Media), Lori Hile (Raintree, 2010)

Websites

How Stuff Works
www.howstuffworks.com
This website explains … well, how stuff works. The web pages are written in simple language. They include information on all sorts of gadgets and are kept up to date.

Greenpeace International
www.greenpeace.org/international/campaigns/toxics/electronics
Greenpeace fills us in on "greener electronics" and offers solutions to businesses and consumers.

Computer Science Lab
www.computersciencelab.com/ComputerHistory/History.htm
This has an illustrated history of computers, with lots of fascinating photographs.

Answers to quizzes

Page 21: a) Eiffel Tower, Paris, France; b) Great Pyramid, Giza, Egypt; c) Taj Mahal, Agra, India.

Page 43: **1** (c), **2** (d), **3** (b), **4** (c), **5** (d), **6** (a), **7** (c), **8** (d).

Topics to investigate

There are many different topics related to handheld gadgets. The websites on page 46 might give some interesting leads. Here are some further research ideas.

Looking back

Imagine what life must have been like in 1950, well before the age of the personal computer and mobile phone. There were not even any pocket calculators. What were the differences in communication? Did they use different forms of communication – written letters, etc.? Put "1950s life" into an internet search engine, and you will find lots of websites to get you started.

Looking forward

What will be the most useful, most fun handheld gadgets in 2050? Will they be very different from the ones mentioned in this book? No one knows, but you can have a guess. Do you think gadgets will continue to get smaller, or is there a point when they are too small to be useful? Make a list of gadgets you would like to see developed. Maybe you could design one or two yourself.

Science

You could research the science behind electronic gadgets. There is some information on the electromagnetic spectrum on page 5 in this book. Put the term into an internet search engine. There is lots more information for you to look at. You could also do further research on electricity.

Security

Security is a serious issue, and you could do further research on aspects such as identity theft. What are the dos and don'ts on the internet?

Index

applications (apps) 14, 16, 37

backup 7
ballpoint pens 35
barcode scanners 38–39
batteries 4, 6, 25, 31
Berners-Lee, Timothy 9
browsers 9

calculators 24–25
camcorders 35
cameras 32–35
co-ordinates 20, 21
computers 4, 6–11, 14
consoles 26, 27
Cooper, Martin 12
cordless phones 17

desktop computers 4, 6
digital assistants 7
digital audio players
    (DAPs) 28
digital cameras (digicams)
    32–33, 34, 35
downloading 29

e-books 14, 30, 31
e-gadgets (electronic
    gadgets) 5
e-readers 30–31
e-waste 18–19
electromagnetic radiation 5
emails 11, 14, 42

fingerprint scanners 39

games 8, 16, 26–27
Global Positioning System
    (GPS) 20, 21, 22–23

hard-disk drives 28, 35
hotspots 10

identity theft 42
infrared radiation 40
internet 6, 8, 9, 10, 14, 16
iPads 8
iPhones 16
iPods 28

Jobs, Steve 8

Land, Edwin 34
laptops 4, 6
live preview 33

megapixels 32
memory cards 28, 32
metal detectors 36, 37, 38
micro-SIMs 15
microchips 5
mobile phones 4, 12–17, 18
mouse 6, 10, 39
MP3 players 28

notebooks 6

palmtop computers 7
personal digital assistants
    (PDAs) 7
personal navigation
    assistants (PNAs) 20
personal organizers 7
phishing 42
photovoltaic cells 25
piracy 29
point and shoot cameras 33
Polaroid cameras 34

QWERTY keyboard 10, 11

radio waves 5, 10, 12, 13, 15,
    22, 40, 41
recycling 18, 19
remote controls 26, 40–41, 41

safety and security 19, 42
satellite phones 17
satellites 14, 17, 20, 22
satnav (satellite navigation)
    20–21
scanners 36–39
security wands 38
Short Message Service
    (SMS) 16
SIM cards 15, 19
smartphones 4, 7, 14, 16–17,
    36, 37, 41
solar cells 25
Sony Walkmans 29
sound waves 36

tablet computers 8
text messages 16, 17
touchpads 6, 10
touchscreens 6, 7, 8, 11, 13,
    27, 30, 41
transistors 5
TV remote controls 40

ultrasound scanners 36

video 14, 17
video cameras 35
videophones 17
viruses 11, 42

walkie-talkies 12
walkthroughs 27
Wi-Fi 10
Wii 26
wireless connection 8, 10
World Wide Web 8, 9

FIND OUT ABOUT
MESOPOTAMIA

COLIN HYNSON

HODDER
Wayland

an imprint of Hodder Children's Books

First published in 2006 by Hodder Wayland,
an imprint of Hodder Children's Books

© Hodder Wayland 2006

Project Editor: Kirsty Hamilton
Designer: Simon Borrough
Maps: Peter Bull

British Library Cataloguing in Publication Data
Hynson, Colin
Find out about Mesopotamia
1. Iraq - Civilization - To 634 - Juvenile literature 2.Iraq
- History - To 634 - Juvenile literature 3. Iraq -
Antiquities - Juvenile literature
I. Title II.Mesopotamia
935

ISBN 07502 47576

Colour Reproduction by Dot Gradations Ltd, UK
Printed in China

Hodder Children's Books
A division of Hodder Headline Limited
338 Euston Road, London NW1 3BH

The publisher would like to thank the following for permission to
reproduce their pictures: Title page, contents, 9, 10, 11, 13, 14, 16, 27, 32,
35, 41, 42, Gianni Dagli Orti / Corbis; 4, Corbis; 6, Nick Wheeler /
Corbis; 7, Archivo Iconografico, S.A./ Corbis; 8, Werner Forman/COR-
BIS; 12, The Art Archive / British Museum;15, 30, Topfoto.co.uk; 18,
Charles & Josette Lenars / Corbis; 19 The Art Archive / Archaeological
Museum Bagdad / Dagli Orti; 20, 22, 23, 24, 25 (right), 26, 31, 43, 44,
TopFoto.co.uk © The British Museum /HIP; 21, Barney Burstein / Corbis;
25 (left), TopFoto.co.uk, HIP / CM Dixon; 28, Silvio Fiore /
Topfoto.co.uk; 29, The Art Archive / Archaeological Museum Aleppo
Syria / Dagli Orti; 33, The Art Archive / Dagli Orti (A); 34, The Art
Archive / Musée du Louvre Paris / Dagli Orti; 36, The Art Archive /
Archaeological Museum Bagdad / Dagli Orti; 37, David Lees / Corbis; 38,
The Art Archive / Musée du Louvre Paris / Dagli Orti (A); 39, Michael S.
Yamashita / Corbis; 40, Topfoto.co.uk © The British Museum / HIP /
Warad –Marduk; 45, Stephanie Sinclair / Corbis

CONTENTS

WHO WERE
THE MESOPOTAMIANS?
4-7

HOW WERE
THE MESOPOTAMIANS
RULED?
8-11

HOW DID
THE MESOPOTAMIANS
EXTEND THEIR RULE?
12-15

WHAT WAS LIFE LIKE
FOR THE MESOPOTAMIANS?
16-31

HOW DID
THE MESOPOTAMIANS
COMMUNICATE?
32-35

WHO DID
THE MESOPOTAMIANS
WORSHIP?
36-41

WHAT DID
THE MESOPOTAMIANS
CONTRIBUTE
TO THE WORLD?
42 45

TIMELINE
FIND OUT MORE
46

GLOSSARY
47

INDEX
48

WHO WERE THE
MESOPOTAMIANS?

When historians talk about the Mesopotamians they are not talking about one group of people or one nation. The word 'Mesopotamia' means 'the land between the rivers'. This refers to land that today can mostly be found in modern-day Iraq with some small parts in Syria and Turkey. The rivers are the great rivers of the Euphrates and the Tigris. From about 3500 BCE the land in-between these rivers gave rise to some of the earliest civilisations in history. The

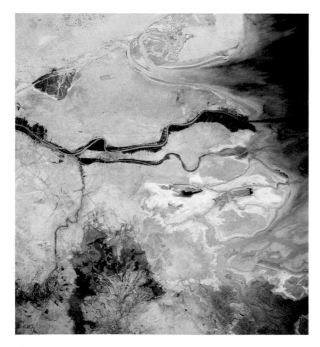

Ʌ A satellite photograph of present-day Iraq, showing the Tigris and Euphrates rivers, which empty into the Persian Gulf.

people in these civilisations are known together as the Mesopotamians.

THE LAND AND CLIMATE

The area of Mesopotamia is dry and hot in the summer and much colder in the winter. There is not very much rainfall at any time of the year. This meant that anybody who lived in this region in ancient times had to be close to the two rivers of the Euphrates and Tigris. Both of the rivers flooded every year between the months of April and June. Like the later ancient Egyptian civilisation, the Mesopotamians relied on the rivers flooding every year to water and feed their crops. If the floods did not happen then the people would go hungry. The rivers occasionally changed course and caused floods where they had never been before. When this happened people had to leave and find a new place to live.

THE MESOPOTAMIAN CIVILISATIONS

There were many different civilisations in Mesopotamia that arose and fell at different periods of history. The dates in which they flourished overlapped and they shared many characteristics. The

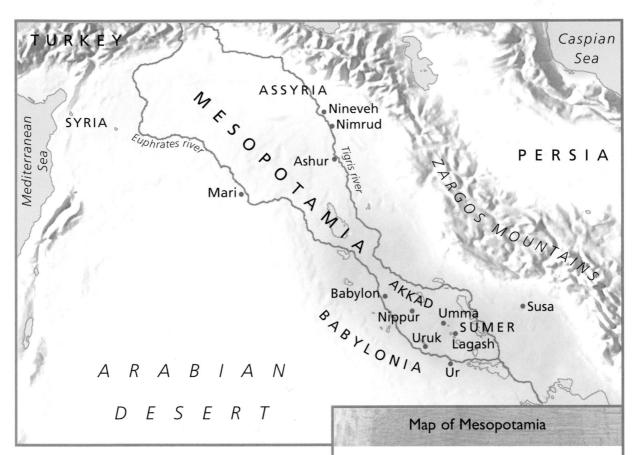

major civilisations were the Chaldeans, Akkadians, and the civilizations covered in this book; the Babylonians, Sumerians and Assyrians.

THE SUMERIANS

In about 3000 BCE, a group of people moved from the north of Mesopotamia to an area south of modern-day Baghdad and inter-married with a local people called the Ubaidians. From these two groups arose a new civilisation called the Sumerians. The first known ruler of the Sumerians was Etana, King of Kish (circa 2800 BCE). In 2300 BCE, the Sumerians were conquered by, and then merged with, the Akkadians. After 2000 BCE, there

WHAT DOES IT TELL US?

This map shows how large an area Mesopotamia was. Although the whole area does not get much rainfall, the north of Mesopotamia does get more than the south. This means that the geography of Mesopotamia does change. This had an impact on the different kinds of civilisation that arose. The lack of rainfall in the south meant that it was far more important that waters of the two rivers were collected for use in agriculture. The northern part of Mesopotamia did not have to spend so long on diverting water onto their crops.

were continual struggles for power which weakened Sumerian civilisation. In the end King Hammurabi became the sole ruler of Sumer. Hammurabi's rise to power marked the end of the Sumerian Empire and the rise of the Babylonians.

THE BABYLONIANS

The Babylonian people occupied land to the south of the city of Baghdad in modern Iraq. They came to occupy the same land as the previous Sumerian civilisation that had begun to fall apart in the 18th century BCE. The Babylonian king, Hammurabi, united and

strengthened the people of his land in this period. The Babylonians adopted many Sumerian traditions such as their artistic styles and architecture. Babylonian civilisation flourished and

Wedding prayer

'Into the Tigris and Euphrates may flood water be brought…May the holy queen of vegetables pile high the grain heaps and mounds.'

WHAT DOES IT TELL US?

This extract from a Babylonian prayer composed in about 2000 BCE was said at a wedding. The prayer refers to the flooding of the two rivers and also to the importance of the floods for farming. It was said at a wedding so that the married couple could share in the crops that would grow because of the flooded rivers.

The ancient site of Uruk

WHAT DOES IT TELL US?

The ancient site of Uruk (shown here) was continually occupied for about 5000 years up until about 300 CE. The size of the remains that can still be seen shows just how large and important cities became in Mesopotamia. This is just one of several large cities that appeared in Mesopotamia.

their ways of life were copied by many of their neighbours. The Babylonian world remained more or less unchanged for the next 1200 years. It was only in 539 BCE that the Persians conquered Babylonia.

The Mesopotamians were a collection of different civilisations that arose in what is now the modern Middle East, and were centred on the area that is the modern country of Iraq. These civilisations began to arise from 4000 BCE. During the next three thousand years, Mesopotamians created the first urban civilisations, invented things like the wheel, writing and number systems and developed large-scale agriculture. After the 5th century BCE the Persians, from modern-day Iran, conquered Mesopotamia. This was the beginning of the end for the Mesopotamian peoples as the Persians imposed their way of life on these newly-conquered lands.

THE ASSYRIANS

The Assyrians lived in the area of modern-day Iraq, which started at about where the modern border between Turkey and Iraq is now and then extended down to near modern Baghdad. This large area that was controlled by the Assyrians was established by king Shamsi-Adad I between 1813 and 1780 BCE. By the middle of the 8th century BCE Assyria had become the most powerful civilisation in Mesopotamia. The Assyrians were seen by other Mesopotamian

Cultivating sugar cane on the bank of the river Tigris

WHAT DOES IT TELL US?
This carving (circa 668-630 BCE) shows crops growing by the edge of one of the two great rivers of ancient Mesopotamia. The crop that is being gathered in is sugar cane, which was a luxury food that could only be afforded by the most wealthy. The river Tigris is represented by waves, fish and swimming figures. This carving makes the river as important as the crop itself and shows how important the rivers were to Mesopotamia's farmers.

societies as being war-like and aggressive. The Assyrian Empire began to fall apart in the 6th century BCE through a series of civil wars and weak rulers.

HOW WERE THE MESOPOTAMIANS RULED?

The Mesopotamian civilisations are generally seen as the first urban societies in history. As more and more people were drawn to live in cities such as Ur, Babylon and Ashur it became necessary to find ways of controlling these large and expanding populations. Large groups of people were seen as threats to the established order. The Mesopotamians were continually fighting each other as well as having to deal with foreign invaders.

All Mesopotamian societies promoted order with strong and central leadership. Mesopotamian leaders saw it as desirable for the people to be organised in a highly structured way, in which everybody knew their place and there were no challenges to the rulers.

MESOPOTAMIAN KINGS

Until King Hammurabi became the monarch of Babylon in 1728 BCE, there are very few details about how the Mesopotamians ruled themselves. It is known that Mesopotamian societies were ruled by kings. The names of the Sumerian kings are known because in about 1800 BCE a 'king list' was written down on a clay tablet. The first kings listed were said to have lived for thousands of years, so some of the names and dates on the tablet are not that reliable. However, the development of writing and written laws in Mesopotamia

Worshippers being led to the king

WHAT DOES IT TELL US?

One of the most powerful and important Sumerian kings was Ur-Nammu who lived from 2112-2095 BCE. This carving (circa 2050 BCE) shows him on his throne, receiving a goddess. She is leading two bare-headed worshippers to him. Mesopotamian kings were not worshipped as gods so the image must be telling us something else. Ur-Nammu built many great temples in the city of Ur and this may show him being thanked for this.

means that there is a lot of information about individual kings in Sumerian, Assyrian and Babylonian cultures.

GOD'S REPRESENTATIVES

In both Babylon and Assyria, kings were often seen as divine. This meant that the main gods chose the kings of these two civilisations. Kings were seen as ruling in the name of the gods. Ruling with the support of the gods made resistance to the king very difficult indeed. Attacking the king would also be an attack on the gods that they worshipped. Assyrian kings acted as high priests and Babylonian kings also took an important part in religious ceremonies.

SARGON II

One of the great Assyrian kings was Sargon II. He reigned from about 722-705 BCE. During his period on the throne of Assyria he extended his rule over numerous states in modern-day Syria and Turkey. He also conquered the ancient kingdom of Israel as far south as Jerusalem. To administer this empire, he created a civil service and appointed governors to rule areas of the empire in his name. To show how powerful he had

Bronze head of Naram-Sin

WHAT DOES IT TELL US?

The bronze head (circa 2250 BCE) of the Assyrian king Naram-Sin is typical of images of Mesopotamian kings. This is because although most Mesopotamian kings were not seen as gods, they liked to model themselves to look like gods. Naram-Sin was the first to believe that he was far more than a king chosen by a god, but was actually a god himself. He called himself the 'king of the universe'.

become Sargon built a new city called Dur Sharrukin, to the north of Nineveh, and had a new palace built there.

HAMMURABI

Hammurabi is one of the best known of the Mesopotamian kings. Hammurabi was king of Babylon between 1728 and 1685 BCE. He built an empire that stretched from the Persian Gulf to the shores of the Mediterranean Sea. Hammurabi became the most powerful king in the region, and Babylon the most important city. He also tried to reign in a way that benefited his people by personally supervising the building of new temples and improving agriculture. He is best remembered for the Code of Hammurabi, a series of laws that governed the lives of his subjects.

∧ This detail from the Stele of Hammurabi (18th century BCE), shows Hammurabi Receiving the Law from the Sun God, Shamash.

The Code of Hammurabi

'Anum and Enlil named me to promote the welfare of the people, me, Hammurabi, the devout, god-fearing prince, to cause justice to prevail in the land, to destroy the wicked and the evil, that the strong should not oppress the weak.'

WHAT DOES IT TELL US?

This quote from the Code of Hammurabi tells us that Hammurabi believed his right to rule came from the gods Anum and Enlil. It also shows us that he believed that he was king for a reason. This was to look after his people and rule well and justly.

THE CODE OF HAMMURABI

The Code of Hammurabi was created at some unknown time during Hammurabi's reign. When the code was introduced, it was the first known time that laws were written down and put on public display. In this way, everybody in the city could know the laws of Babylon. Part of the code's job was also to set out the way that Babylonian society was supposed to be structured.

Many of the laws that are part of the Code of Hammurabi were designed to protect the most vulnerable and weak members of Babylonian society from the most powerful by making sure that all were equally protected by the law. It laid out what punishments would be given for different crimes. These included penalties for surgeons who carried out unsuccessful operations and fines for neglect in various trades. The punishments for crimes against people and property were based on the idea of 'an eye for an eye'. The general rule was that, for example, if somebody broke another person's bone then the offender's punishment would be to have the same bone broken.

⋏ This carving from throne of Shalmaneser III, shows a detail of Shalmaneser III and King Markud-zakir-shumi

Proud kings

'I am Shalmaneser, the legitimate king, the king of the world, the king without rival…overlord of all the princes, who has smashed all his enemies as if they were earthenware.'

WHAT DOES IT TELL US?

Shalmaneser III was an Assyrian king. He reigned from 859-824 BCE. During his reign the Assyrian Empire continued to expand. Mesopotamian kings often wrote boastful things about themselves, to help justify their rule over people.

BABYLONIAN SOCIETY

The Code of Hammurabi divided Babylonian society into three classes: the *amelu*, the *muskinu* and the *ardu*. The *amelu* were the ruling class of Babylon, including the king and court, senior government officials and wealthy professionals. The code does not make it clear who the *muskinu* were. It appears that they were landless workers. This does not necessarily mean that they were poor. The *muskinu* and *amelu* were supposed to live separately from each other. The *ardu* were slaves. Slaves were protected under the code. They were allowed to buy their freedom, own property, and even own their own slaves.

HOW DID THE MESOPOTAMIANS EXTEND THEIR RULE?

The fertile plains of Mesopotamia, along with the wealth of the great cities, meant that war was a constant feature of Mesopotamian history as different tribes and states fought for control of these riches. The first record of warfare in the region comes from around 3000 BCE. Images from Uruk and Susa show scenes of fighting and of prisoners of war kneeling in front of kings. From then on Mesopotamia was rarely at

The Royal Standard of Ur

WHAT DOES IT TELL US?
This section from the Royal Standard of Ur has images of the Sumerian army. It dates from about 2600-2400 BCE. These pictures detail how professionally Sumerian soldiers were dressed and what kinds of weapons they had. Both spears and swords are seen being carried into battle. It also reveals the use of horses and chariots in both, taking part in the battle and also transporting weapons.

peace. There was fighting for power and territory between different parts of Mesopotamia as well as fighting between Mesopotamians and external invaders such as the Persians.

THE FIRST ARMIES

As the Mesopotamians began to organise themselves into more complex societies they began to think of better ways to defend themselves. One of the ways of doing this was to form armies. A king called Sargon the Great ruled over the Akkadians from about 2335-2279 BCE. During his reign he conquered virtually the whole of Mesopotamia. He did this not just because opposition to him never united against him, but also because of the way he organised his army. For the first time, an army of full-time soldiers was created. Before this, armies were created from local people who were brought together to fight a war and sent home again when the fighting stopped. Sargon the Great raised an army of about 10,000 permanent soldiers who were properly trained and equipped. Because Sargon had to defeat enemies who defended themselves from behind the walls of cities, he also developed new kinds of weapons for sieges, such as battering rams.

THE ASSYRIAN EMPIRE

Around the end of the 10th century BCE Assyria began to expand. From 1200 BCE onwards, however, Assyria had to continually defend itself from outside attack. It did this successfully by building an army that would become known throughout Mesopotamia as one of the most ruthless ever seen. The Assyrian king Tiglath-Pileser III, who reigned from 745-727 BCE, wanted control over the whole of Mespotamia and beyond. He created a permanent army that was mostly made up of non-Assyrians. He defeated the Babylonians and conquered parts of modern-day Syria, Turkey and Israel. One of the ways that he kept rule over these lands was to move an entire population of conquered people to different parts of the empire so that they could not get together and rebel against Assyrian rule.

Assyrian chariot

WHAT DOES IT TELL US?

This stone carving shows an Assyrian chariot going into battle. It dates from about 800 BCE. The carving confirms that chariots were usually ridden by two soldiers. One soldier had the job of steering the chariot and the other soldier did the fighting.

WEAPONS AND ARMOUR

Early Mesopotamian weapons were the same as those used for hunting, like spears, clubs and bows and arrows. From 3000 BCE onwards new weapons made of metal, such as swords and axes, began to appear. These were normally made of copper or bronze. After 2000 BCE weapons made of iron gradually replaced these softer metals.

From 2000 BCE the use of horses in war also began to change. Before this date they were mostly used to carry weapons and other equipment. Then, horses began to be used for fighting as the idea of a cavalry began to develop. Horses were either ridden by soldiers or were

▷ This wall painting (circa 522-486 BCE), shows an Archer of the Royal Guard of Darius I, king of Persia.

Herodotus quote

'The Assyrians went to war with helmets upon their heads made of brass…They carried shields, lances and daggers, very much like the Egyptians.'

WHAT DOES IT TELL US?

This quote comes from the 5th century BCE Greek historian Herodotus. Texts like this help to confirm what kinds of weapons the ancient Assyrians carried with them when they went into battle. Texts are even more useful if the information they give is also found on paintings and carvings.

A cavalry charge

What does it tell us?

This relief carving from the 9th century BCE comes from the palace of Kalhu. The relief helps us to understand how Mesopotamian soldiers may have fought on horseback. None of the horses have a saddle or stirrups. The soldiers are shown wearing helmets and using long spears and bow and arrows as weapons.

used to pull chariots. These chariots were fast and light and could carry a maximum of four archers.

To protect themselves Mesopotamian soldiers would normally wear leather or metal helmets on their heads. Their armour would be made of tiny pieces of bronze that overlapped each other, like the scales of a fish, which were then sewn onto a tunic.

INVADING MESOPOTAMIA

The states that bordered Mesopotamia remained a threat to the states between the two rivers of the Tigris and the Euphrates. The main rivals of the Mesopotamians came from the east. In about 1500 BCE, in what is now modern-day Iran, the Persian kingdom arose. In 558 BCE Cyrus the Great took the throne of Persia and began to expand his empire. In 546 BCE he conquered Lydia, a country in modern-day Turkey. He then turned his sights towards Mesopotamia. Cyrus the Great attacked and in 539 BCE he conquered Babylonia. Mesopotamia remained under Persian rule until 331 BCE when Alexander the Great drove the Persians out.

WHAT WAS LIFE LIKE FOR THE MESOPOTAMIANS?

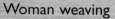
Woman weaving

WHAT DOES IT TELL US?

This terracotta relief plaque (circa 2000 BCE) shows a woman weaving. This tells us that spinning and weaving was generally done by women in Mesopotamia. It was an important source of income, even for homes that could afford a servant.

The everyday lives of the people of Mesopotamia are difficult to uncover. Historians and archaeologists rely on written and physical evidence to find out about past civilisations. For Mesopotamian societies there is very little evidence on the lives of ordinary people. There is more evidence on the lives of the wealthy and privileged. This is because it is more likely that objects they owned would survive to the present day as they were better made.

Any writings about people's lives that have survived are much more likely to be about those at the top of Mesopotamian society.

THE LIVES OF MESOPOTAMIAN WOMEN

The lives led by women in Mesopotamian society were strictly defined in terms of their role in the family. A Mesopotamian woman was seen as a daughter, wife or mother, and they were very rarely seen outside of the confines of their families. If they were, they tended to be royal women or those with rich and powerful husbands. Mesopotamian women were required to be responsible for their homes. Indeed, not keeping a well-ordered house was regarded as a good reason for divorce. The fact that this is seen as a woman's domain is one reason why we don't know very much about Mesopotamian homes, because it was not seen as important by those who recorded Mesopotamian life.

WOMEN'S RIGHTS

At no point in Mesopotamian history was it believed that men and women had equal rights. However, from early on in Mesopotamian history women were free to go out to the marketplace, buy and sell goods, borrow and lend money, engage in business and attend to their husband's legal matters. Several contracts involving women running their own businesses have been found. Some women, such as the high priestess of the temple of the Goddess Bau, had a lot of power. According to a document from around 2350 BCE, the priestess was in charge of the temple and of the 1000 people who worked there throughout the year.

WOMEN AND THE CODE OF HAMMURABI

Babylonian women had only limited protection under the Code of Hammurabi. Married women could easily be divorced for virtually any reason, including childlessness or even poor household management. All the husband had to do was to say 'You are not my wife' and return her dowry (property given by the wife's family to the husband's family when they get married). Under the code, any woman who tried to do the same thing could be drowned. A woman could not divorce her husband but she was able to leave him if she could prove cruelty or if he made a false accusation against her.

Women's rights

'If a woman quarrels with her husband…the reasons for her prejudice must be presented. If she is guiltless, and there is no fault on her part, but he leaves and neglects her, then no guilt attaches to this woman, she shall take her dowry and go back to her father's house.'

WHAT DOES IT TELL US?

This is a part of the Code of Hammurabi. Men were allowed to divorce their wives for the most trivial of reasons. This part of the code shows that women also had permission to no longer live with their husbands if they were falsely accused of something or if they could prove 'cruelty'. However, they were not allowed to divorce.

A FAMOUS MESOPOTAMIAN WOMAN

Although there are few details of individual women from ancient Mespotamia, one of the best-known women from that time was Enheduanna. She was the daughter of Sargon, the king of the Akkadians. She was the chief priestess of the Moon-God temple in Ur around 2300 BCE. Enheduanna is now the earliest known female poet in the world. Her poetry about the gods and goddesses was very popular at the time.

INSIDE AN ORDINARY MESOPOTAMIAN HOME

Archaeological evidence shows that ordinary people lived in small, cube-shaped houses. These usually had two floors. On the ground floor there would be workshops and an area for receiving guests. The living quarters were on the next floor. There was also an open courtyard where the family could cook, eat and relax together. Few families could afford their own bathrooms and toilets. For those that could buy them, drains were built which emptied into a nearby river. Most houses were built of sun-dried bricks made from mud. These helped keep houses cool in the summer. The frame was sometimes painted red to ward off evil spirits.

A Mesopotamian palace

WHAT DOES IT TELL US?

This picture shows the remains of the palace of Nebuchadnezzar II (630-562 BCE) in Babylon. Even though it is now in ruins the picture shows the scale of the palace. It is also known as the site of the 'Hanging Gardens of Babylon', which the Greek writer Philo called one of the seven wonders of the ancient world. There is still some debate about whether the gardens actually existed or not.

ROYAL RESIDENCES

There is a lot more evidence about palaces, the homes of the kings of ancient Mesopotamia. These were also built of sun-dried mud bricks and were two stories high, but the similarities ended there. Some of the palaces were huge, with as many as 300 rooms. These rooms had all sorts of functions including storing treasure or serving as workshops for craftsmen. Nebuchadnezzar II built the most famous royal palace in Babylon. Sometime between 630-562 BCE he is believed to have built the 'Hanging Gardens' at his palace. These were plants and trees that were built high up the palace walls and could be seen to be hanging down.

MESOPOTAMIAN FASHION

Only a few fragments of Mesopotamian clothing have survived to the present day. All of the information

about what Mesopotamian men and women wore comes from sculptures, metalwork and designs on seals (a carved stamp used to mark documents).

Beginning in about 3000 BCE men are shown bare-chested with a knee or ankle-length skirt that is tied at the waist. They also wore a headband called a *fillet*. Women wore a plain knee-length robe that was draped over the left shoulder, with the right shoulder and arm left uncovered. They also wore shawls that they fastened by pins decorated with beads.

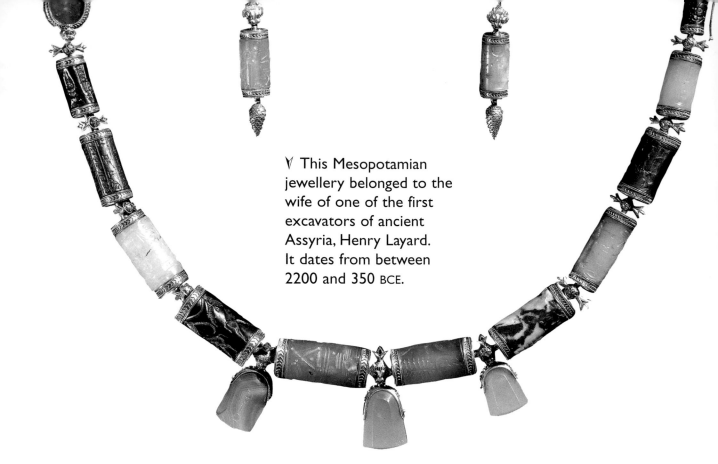

▼ This Mesopotamian jewellery belonged to the wife of one of the first excavators of ancient Assyria, Henry Layard. It dates from between 2200 and 350 BCE.

Artefacts show that there seems to be only small differences between the clothing of rich and poor Mesopotamians. However, wealthier Mesopotamians made sure that their clothing was slightly different either by using materials of brighter colours or by adding some jewellery.

CHANGING FASHIONS

Early Mesopotamian clothing for both men and women was usually made from the skins of sheep and goats. Later, cloth was woven from a plant called flax. Flax cloth was easy to work into different thicknesses so that clothes could be made for either the winter or summer. The clothing worn by both men and women changed very little for several centuries. From about 2300 BCE, the robes became less plain and decorations were added.

One of the Mesopotamian fashions that did change was whether men wore beards. Images from 3000 BCE show all men wearing long beards. One thousand years later, the images have changed. Some men still had beards but others were clean-shaven. Priests are shown without beards and with shaven heads.

MESOPOTAMIAN JEWELLERY

Both men and women in Mesapotamia wore earrings and necklaces. During celebrations, even more jewellery was

WHAT DOES IT TELL US?

This gold headdress (circa 2600 BCE) is the Sumerian Gold Jewellery of Queen Shubad of Ur. It shows us that Mesopotamia had skilled craftspeople. The gold leaves had to be hammered to the right thickness and then made into the right shapes. A similar headdress was found at the Royal Cemetery at Ur. It is not known whether it was worn by somebody in life or whether it was especially made when they died so that it could be worn in the coffin.

worn. The wealthier Mesopotamians often wore beautiful gold and silver bracelets and earrings. Necklaces were also worn and were set with bright, precious stones, including lapis lazuli and carnelian.

MESOPOTAMIAN METALWORK

Bronze, copper and tin were common metals in Mesopotamia. They were used to make household goods as well as weapons and parts for chariots. The Mesopotamians are seen by modern historians as skilled metalworkers. Many of the pieces of metal found at the Royal Cemetery of Ur show metalwork of the highest standard of craftsmanship. The gold and silver objects in the cemetery show that the Mesopotamians who worked with these precious metals were as skilled as anyone else in the world at the time. One of the main problems the Mesopotamians faced was that very little metal naturally occurred where they lived. The metal that they used had to be brought in from other countries. It is believed that the gold they used came from the area that is now modern-day Turkey. Some metals, like iron and copper, could be found locally.

MESOPOTAMIAN GLASS

One of the greatest achievements of the Mesopotamians was the invention of glass. It is believed by most archaeologists that glass was first created in about 3000 BCE in Mesopotamia. The earliest objects made from glass were beads. In about 1500 BCE, the Mesopotamians discovered how to make hollow glass vessels such as bottles and vases. Glass production continued until about 1200 BCE when it mysteriously disappeared. It emerged again in about 900 BCE.

Mesopotamian glassware

WHAT DOES IT TELL US?

This blue glass bottle comes from the Kassite dynasty and dates from between 1300 and 1200 BCE. It was found in a grave at Ur. The bottle was made only a few hundred years after the Mesopotamians had learnt how to make hollow glass objects. It enabled them to make containers that were not only very practical but also beautiful. The Mesopotamians also discovered how to colour glass. Cobalt was added to the molten glass to make a blue colour. Antimony made white glass and copper was used for making green glass.

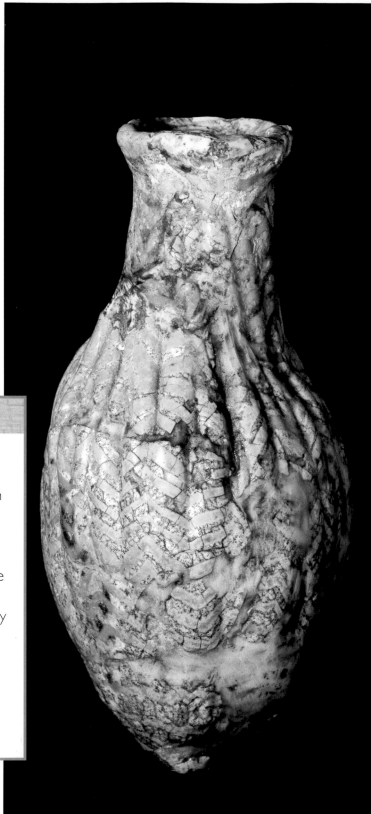

WHAT DOES IT TELL US?

This piece of Mesopotamian pottery from around the 8th or 7th century BCE, shows us that clay pots were being made on a potter's wheel. It also shows us that the Mesopotamians had learnt how to put a glaze on their pots. The glaze made the pots stronger, waterproof, and also helped to decorate the surface. The earliest glazed pots date from around 1500 BCE. Glaze was also used on decorated brickwork.

MESOPOTAMIAN POTTERY

Clay, the main material of pottery, could be found across many different parts of Mesopotamia. As in many other parts of the ancient world, potters used their fingers to shape their clay. There is evidence that from about 4500 BCE potters in Mesopotamia began to use wheels that they turned with their legs to make pottery.

WORKING IN STONE

The Mesopotamians were also skilled at carving sculptures. Many of their stone figures are either of gods and goddesses, or of kings and other important people like priests. Ordinary people are represented in these carvings but are only shown serving their king. Mesopotamian carvers were well-known for carving figures in relief. These were flat carvings made of alabaster that could be placed onto walls or gates. Statues were also made out of marble and limestone.

Moving a statue

WHAT DOES IT TELL US?

This picture comes from the wall of the palace of the Assyrian King Sennacherib (704-681 BCE) at Nineveh. It shows us how statues were transported. The statue in the picture is not yet finished. It has been placed on wooden rollers and is being pulled along by prisoners. The prisoners are being guarded by soldiers whilst they are working. The soldiers are probably there to prevent the prisoners from escaping.

CHILDREN'S TOYS

Excavations by archaeologists at burial sites in Mesopotamia show that the Mesopotamian children could enjoy themselves in lots of different ways. Toy animals, wooden balls and rattles have been found at the graves of Mesopotamian children. However, toys were only for the children of wealthy people. Most children probably did not have any kind of toys, and instead worked from an early age.

WHAT DOES IT TELL US?

This is a pull-along toy for a Mesopotamian child dating from the 12th century BCE. The hedgehog is made from limestone and the cart is made from stone. There was another animal behind the hedgehog. It shows us that children did have toys to play with. However, any toy at this time would have been expensive, so only the wealthiest children were given things to play with.

MUSIC

It will never be known what Mesopotamian music sounded like in its time. However, Mesopotamian music had an important part in their religious and personal lives. After 2000 BCE the Sumerians began to build new temples in their cities. Texts left behind show us that hymns to their gods were sung in these temples, with some parts being sung by a priest and some by a choir.

The Royal lyre

WHAT DOES IT TELL US?

This lyre was found in the grave of Queen Pu-abi at the Royal Cemetery at Ur. It dates from about 2600–2400 BCE. The fact that this lyre was put in a grave shows us just how important music was to the Mesopotamians. This lyre was made from the finest materials including gold. This would have made it very expensive and again shows us the importance of music in Mesopotamia.

Excavations at various tombs have revealed the remains of musical instruments such as flutes, drums, lyres, reed pipes and harps. The Mesopotamians were also the first people to write down their music and write about how to play the instruments that they had.

PLAYING BOARD GAMES

In the 1920s an archaeologist called Sir Leonard Wooley excavated some tombs in the ancient Sumerian city of Ur. What he discovered in these royal tombs has helped to create a much fuller picture of life in ancient Mesopotamia. Many of the best known Mesopotamian artefacts were discovered by Wooley including the Standard of Ur, a decorated box showing scenes of Sumerian life, and many of the finest examples of metalsmithing.

The Royal game of Ur board

WHAT DOES IT TELL US?

This board game is one of the best-known Mesopotamian pieces in the British Museum, London, dating from 26 to 24 BCE. The rules for the game were written down and still survive. The rules are quite complicated so it is clearly a game to be played by adults. The expensive materials used to make the board and the quality of the workmanship shows that it could only have been used by somebody with plenty of money.

Amongst the treasures that he found were two board games. Together they are called the 'Royal Game of Ur'. The games date from about 2600 BCE. Another simpler board game has also been found at the tomb of Queen Shub-ad, about five hundred miles from Ur. Today, the British Museum website has an online version of the Royal Game of Ur.

FARMING AND FOOD

The area of land that the Mesopotamians occupied has been called the 'fertile crescent'. This land was one of the first places in the world to be farmed.

Preparing food

WHAT DOES IT TELL US?

This stone carving comes from the palace of King Ashurnasirpal (883-859 BCE). It shows servants preparing a meal for the king. It tells us that Mesopotamians were able to prepare and cook complex meals and that food was very important to them. One servant is waving a fan over the food. He is doing this either to cool it down or to keep flies off the food.

Animals such as sheep were domesticated in Mesopotamia beginning in about 9000 BCE and crops were grown about one thousand years later. As Mesopotamian cities began to expand, improvements in farming had to be made to feed this urban population.

WHAT DID THE MESOPOTAMIANS EAT?

For many Mesopotamians, the most important food was bread. Because they did not grow much wheat, most of their bread was made from barley grains that were ground into flour. Mesopotamians added milk, cheese, dried fruit and seeds to their bread to give it a bit of extra flavour. They also used barley to brew a weak beer. This was drunk through a straw to avoid any bits of barley that would be floating on the surface of the beer.

Seeds like lentils, peas, chickpeas and broad beans were a very important part of the Mesopotamian diet and were either eaten raw or cooked. Some seeds such as alfalfa were cultivated for animal fodder.

➢ This ancient Babylonian mill, used for grinding flour, still stands in modern-day Iraq.

The main vegetables grown and eaten by Mesopotamians were garlic, leeks, onions and cucumbers. Fruits like apples, figs, pears and dates were grown and eaten. Lettuce and radishes were also eaten but were brought in from ancient Egypt.

Most of the meat eaten by Mesopotamians came from their farm animals such as cattle, goats and sheep. However, the Mesopotamians also ate food that had been hunted. They fished in the Tigris and Euphrates rivers and in the Mediterranean Sea and Persian Gulf.

Hunting animals

WHAT DOES IT TELL US?

This terracotta seal comes from around 2000 BCE and was found in the city of Mari in modern-day Syria. Although farmers in Mesopotamia reared animals such as goats and sheep, this seal shows that they may have looked after animals that are not normally found on a farm. The seal shows deer being looked after by a man and dog. The deer might have been released from the farm for hunting.

Fish was considered a great delicacy. There is also evidence that Mesopotamians hunted and ate wild animals such as deer.

MESOPOTAMIAN FARMING

The area of Mesopotamia was so large that farmers in different parts of the region had to develop different ways of growing their crops and looking after their animals. The main differences between regions had to do with varying soil quality and weather in the north and south of Mesopotamia.

A farmer's instructions

'When you are about to cultivate your field, take care to open the irrigation works so that their water does not rise too high in the field.'

WHAT DOES IT TELL US?

This instruction to farmers comes from about 1700 BCE on a clay tablet. It shows us that the collection and storage of water was very important to Mesopotamian farmers. It also shows us that farmers were able to control the amount of water they let flow on to their fields.

Irrigation canals

WHAT DOES IT TELL US?

On the plains of southern Mesopotamia, irrigation canals built thousands of years ago can still be seen. The picture, from Assur, Iraq, shows us that the canals were a major piece of engineering that needed to be constantly maintained in order to work properly. Some of the canals are still used today.

In the north, farmers had enough rainfall to water their crops. However, the south of Mesopotamia received far less rainfall. The Tigris and Euphrates rivers flooded each year between April and June. However the floods did not happen at the time when farmers needed the water. This meant they needed a way to control and store the water until it was needed. This problem was solved by the digging of irrigation canals. These canals were designed to channel the flood waters away from the fields. The water could then be stored in these canals until it was needed to feed the crops.

These irrigation canals regularly filled up with silt from the rivers so it was important that they were kept clear. It was seen as the duty of all Mesopotamians to make sure that these canals were kept free of silt by digging it out. If the flood waters were not collected then the crops would fail and there would be famine.

THE GROWING YEAR

In Mesopotamia the agricultural season began in late October or November when the land was ploughed and the seeds were then sown. This meant that the seeds were growing in the early spring and this is when the flood water was needed the most. Harvesting of the ripened crop took place from the end of April and went on until June.

Cylinder seal showing agricultural statistics

WHAT DOES IT TELL US?

This is a cylinder seal from the Sumerian city of Ur and dates from about 2000-1900 BCE. The writing of the seal has a remarkable amount of detail about field sizes, barley yields and other aspects of farming. Archaeologists have discovered many thousands of these kind of seals. These seals tell us that Mesopotamian rulers wanted to record how much food was being produced in their kingdoms. They also give modern archaeologists information on Mesopotamian agriculture.

HOW DID THE MESOPOTAMIANS COMMUNICATE?

One of the great achievements of the Mesopotamians was the invention of writing. Writing meant that Mesopotamian civilisations could make much greater progress. Ideas and decisions could be passed on from one generation to the next and need never be forgotten. It also means that historians can learn a lot more about the life of the Mesopotamians through their own words. The writing that has been left behind ranges from the laws of the Babylonians through to stories and lists of crops grown on farms.

Writing on clay

WHAT DOES IT TELL US?

This Sumerian clay tablet with a tally of sheep, is an example of the cuneiform script. Many of these tablets were put inside a second clay case to make sure that the contents of the tablets were not interfered with before the message reached the hands of the person who was supposed to receive it. The text itself would either be read from the left to right or from top to bottom. This depended on which way the scribe wrote the cuneiform text.

WRITING WITH PICTURES

Like other early civilisations the first kind of writing used by the Mesopotamians used pictures to represent a word. These symbols are called *pictographs*. A picture of a fish meant one fish. If a fish had two circles next to it then it meant two fishes. This kind of writing was usually used by farmers to keep records of their animals and crops. Pictographs were limited because they could only be used to write about objects. This way of writing also meant that a lot of pictograms had to be memorised in order to read and write properly.

Necklace bead

WHAT DOES IT TELL US?

This necklace bead dates from about 2500 BCE and belonged to Mesanepada, the King of Hur Mari. The scratches on the surface of the bead are cuneiform inscriptions. It was not just clay tablets that were used for writing on. Any hard surface could be used as well. The cuneiform words would be scratched or carved in rather than pressed into a softer material.

WRITING WITH SYMBOLS

A new way of writing was created by the Sumerians in around 3000 BCE. The pictures of objects were replaced with symbols for each word, allowing written words for things that were not objects and making it possible for words in the Sumerian language to be written. This kind of writing is known as *phonographs*.

WRITING WITH LETTERS

Between 1700 BCE and 1500 BCE the world's first alphabet was developed in ancient Palestine and Syria. In an alphabet, one symbol or letter represents one sound rather than an entire word. Alphabetic writing is simpler to read than earlier forms, because all people had to do was learn the symbols for the small number of sounds that make up spoken words rather than memorise a large number of unique symbols. By about 1000 BCE the Mesopotamians began to create their own alphabet using a form of cuneiform writing.

The Code of Hammurabi

WHAT DOES IT TELL US?

Mesopotamian laws were written down so that everybody could read them. This picture shows the block of black basalt stone into which was carved the Code of Hammurabi in the 18th century BCE. The stone is over two metres tall and weighs about 4 tonnes. It shows how Babylonian laws were communicated to the people in a public place. People who could read would be asked to call out what was written on the stone.

WRITING ON CLAY

The Mesopotamians did not write on paper or even on papyrus like the ancient Egyptians. They wrote on soft clay tablets. This was done by holding a piece of soft clay in one hand. The top of the clay was flattened, then the words were written by pressing a stylus into the clay to leave a mark. The stylus was normally made from the stem of a water reed. When the writing was finished the clay was dried and the writing became permanent. The characters written on this kind of tablet looked like a series of wedge-shaped marks. This kind of writing is known as *cuneiform*, which comes from the Latin word for 'wedge'. Using these wedges also meant that it was easier to carve words into stone. Cuneiform was used when the Code of Hammurabi was inscribed onto blocks of stone so that people could read it.

CYLINDER SEALS

One of the ways that the Mesopotamians would communicate with each other was through the use of cylinder seals. These seals were invented in around 3500 BCE in southern Mesopotamia. They were about 3cm long. A hole through the middle of the cylinder allowed it to be carried around using a string or a pin. The seals were usually made of stone but could also be made from wood, bone, shell, ivory or metal. Cuneiform words and pictures were carved into the surface of the seal. This could then be rolled out onto soft clay tablets to leave a continuous impression. These tablets were often used by merchants to mark their goods and to record agreements between them.

Cylinder seals

WHAT DOES IT TELL US?

Cylinder seals varied in many ways. They were made of different materials like stone or wood and could be different sizes. However, this Uruk seal (circa 4000-2000 BCE) shows how all cylinder seals worked. The seal was placed on a piece of soft clay and then rolled over it. When the seal was taken off it left behind an impression of the image that had been carved into the seal.

WHO DID THE MESOPOTAMIANS WORSHIP?

The Mesopotamians worshipped many different gods and goddesses. Belief in many different gods and goddesses is known as polytheism. These gods and goddesses had different names in different cities. Their names also changed over time. The main god of Babylon was Marduk. The people of the city of Ashur had a god called Ashur. People in cities chose one of these gods to be their special *city god*.

SOME SUMERIAN GODS

The Sumerians had four major gods, who were known as the creating gods. These gods were An, the god of heaven; Ki, the goddess of earth; Enlil, the god of air and Enki the god of water. Heaven, earth, air and water were seen as the main elements of everything in the universe.

Below these gods were some lesser deities. There were three sky gods and goddesses. These were Nanna, the god of the moon; Utu, the god of the sun and Innana, the queen of heaven. Innana was also the goddess of love and war.

Making an offering

WHAT DOES IT TELL US?

This limestone plaque dates from about 2500-2300 BCE. It comes from the city of Ur in southern Mesopotamia and shows a religious procession in progress. It reveals information about religious processions and festivals in Mesopotamia such as how the people lined up and presented offerings. At the front of both lines of people an offering is being made to the seated god being worshipped. It appears that the people are offering cloth to the gods.

Below these lesser deities were also many minor gods and goddesses. There were gods for rivers and mountains, fields and farms and even of tools like axes, ploughs and brick moulds.

WORSHIPPING GODS

The Mesopotamians, like many other ancient peoples, believed that the gods and goddesses played an active part in their everyday lives. All the Mesopotamian civilisations, from Sumerian, to Babylonian, to Assyrian, believed it was important to worship the gods on a regular basis, particularly when asking for something.

Much of the worship took place in temples with priests leading. The priests composed hymns to praise the gods and goddesses and to thank them for what they had done already. Both the priest and any worshippers in the temple usually sang these hymns.

Worshipping statues

WHAT DOES IT TELL US?
These Sumerian statues (circa 2700 BCE) come from the Square Temple at Eshnunna. They are meant to represent people praying. The fact that they were found at a temple tells us that they were probably left as offerings. It is believed that the statues were left to pray perpetually once the worshippers had left the temple.

RELIGIOUS FESTIVALS

During the year there were certain days that were put aside as special holy days or festivals. During the city festivals the city gods and goddesses were praised. In return it was hoped that the gods and goddesses would protect the people and the cities they lived in. Many of these festivals were linked to important moments in the farming calendar. One example of this was the festival of *akitu* which was a time to thank the gods for the barley harvest.

Statue of Gilgamesh

WHAT DOES IT TELL US?

The *Epic of Gilgamesh* was one of the best-known stories to come out of Mespotamia. The stories were written down by the Sumerians in about 2000 BCE. This statue of Gilgamesh dates from about 800 BCE, over one thousand years later. The date of the statue shows us that the story was one that was very important throughout Mesopotamian history.

TEMPLES

Temples could be found in every town and city in Mesopotamia. In the larger and more important cities there were several temples in which the gods and goddesses could be worshipped. However, there was always one temple that was more important than all of the others. This was the temple used to worship the god that was supposed to protect the city. For example, the Sumerian city of Lagash had a temple built to their city goddess, Baba.

THE TEMPLE BUILDING

Temples in Mesopotamia were not thought of as just a place where people went to worship and to make offerings to the gods. It was believed that the gods actually lived in the temples. There were also rooms for the priests, courtyards for public worship and storage areas for valuables such as gold and jewellery and for barley. Barley was one of the most important crops in Mesopotamia and was used to make both beer and bread. A high wall surrounded the whole of the temple to separate it from the rest of the city.

THE ZIGGURAT

The best-known type of Mesopotamian temple was called a *ziggurat*. The word *ziggurat* comes from an Assyrian word meaning 'pinnacle'. They were built between 4000 BCE and 600 BCE. Sixteen ziggurats have been excavated by archaeologists and others are known about from various texts. There are remains of ziggurats at Ur, Uruk and Nippur.

The structure of these ziggurats followed a common pattern. They are pyramid-shaped with several flat platforms built on top of each other. At the top of the ziggurat was a temple. The pyramid had steps around the outside which led to the top. It was a solid structure with no rooms or passages inside. The most

The Ziggurat at Ur

WHAT DOES IT TELL US?
This ziggurat in the ancient city of Ur, known today as Tell al-Muqayyar, dates from around 2000 BCE. It was reconstructed in the 1920s and 1930s by the British archaeologist, Sir Leonard Woolley, to make it appear as it would have looked when it was first built. It shows us how a ziggurat was designed. Separate levels were built on top of each other and the temple was placed on the top. The long staircases were almost certainly an important part of religious processions as they could accommodate a long line of people.

WHAT DOES IT TELL US?

This clay mask represents the demon Humbaba. It comes from Sippar, which is in the south of Mesopotamia, and it dates from about 1800-1600 BCE. Humbaba makes an appearance in the Epic of Gilgamesh. Like other demons Humbaba is part-human and part-animal. This mask shows us that Humbaba's face was supposed to have appeared like animal intestines.

famous ziggurat of all was built in Babylon and was dedicated to the god Marduk. It was this ziggurat that inspired the story of the Tower of Babel that is mentioned in the Bible.

DEMONS AND MONSTERS

The Mesopotamians did not just believe in the existence of gods and goddesses, they also believed in demons, spirits, ghosts and other supernatural beings.

A prayer

'From the land of the rising to the land of the setting sun.
O mountain, Lord of life, you are indeed Lord!
O Bel of the lands, Lord of life you yourself are Lord of life.
O mighty one, terrible one of heaven, you are guardian indeed!
O Bel, you are Lord of the gods indeed!'

WHAT DOES IT TELL US?

This prayer dates from around 1600 BCE. What it shows us is that when the Mesopotamians were praying they were not always asking for something from the gods. Various writings tell us that the Mesopotamians believed that the gods had to be praised both before and after praying for favours. This prayer is directed to the god Bel.

These demons took on many forms, usually a mixture of human and animal. They also took on the personalities of people and animals. One of the most common demonic images is of a man with wings or with eagle heads or cloaks made of fish. These demons were believed to be responsible for all sorts of misfortunes and Mesopotamians believed they needed to pray to the gods to avoid them.

MESOPOTAMIAN MYTHOLOGY

The most famous Mesopotamian myth is the Epic of Gilgamesh. It was written in cuneiform on twelve clay tablets around 2000 BCE. It tells the story of a Babylonian king called Gilgamesh. His subjects prayed to be released from his oppressive rule. The gods sent a wild man called Enkidu to fight Gilgamesh. The fight ended in a draw and the two of them became friends and shared many adventures. They returned to Gilgamesh's palace where Enkidu died and Gilgamesh left to find a plant that would give him eternal youth. He lost the plant to a serpent and he returned to his home to end his days.

≺ A statue of the demon Pazuzu (circa 700 BCE).

WHAT DID THE MESOPOTAMIANS CONTRIBUTE TO THE WORLD?

The Mesopotamian civilisations have left behind a legacy that still remains with us today. Many of their stories and buildings have some similarities with stories that can be found in the Bible. The story of Ut-napishtim is about the world being deluged in a great flood. The main temple in Babylon is seen as the source for the Tower of Babel. Even the three wise men from the East that travelled to Bethlehem were thought to be Mesopotamian astronomers. However, it is in three main areas that Mesopotamian achievements are still with us today. These are transport, mathematics and astronomy.

TRANSPORT

The Mesopotamians have been credited with inventing one of the most important objects in history, the wheel. The first wheels appeared in Mesopotamia in about 3000 BCE. They were solid wheels that were made from several wooden planks that were shaped into discs and held together with metal bands. About one thousand years later, wheels with spokes began to appear.

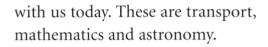
Wheeled transport

WHAT DOES IT TELL US?

This model of a chariot comes from the city of Ur and dates from around 2000 BCE. It tells us about the design and shape of chariots in Mesopotamia around this time. There is a seat at the front for the driver and the area at the back was used for transporting goods. The wheels are solid rather than made with spokes. This can help historians to work out when the model was made.

WHAT DOES IT TELL US?

The granite weight in the shape of a duck dates from about 2000 BCE. It comes from Ur at a time when the city was becoming more powerful. These weights have been found throughout the city. This shows us that weighing and measuring in Ur was becoming standardised so that everybody used the same ways to weigh and measure things. This weight is 2 *talents*. A talent is about 30 kilograms and was divided into 60 *minas*.

Transport using wheels also led to the development of roads between towns and cities. It made communication quicker and easier and allowed armies to be moved around quickly. The arrival of the wheel was a major advance for human civilisation. It is very difficult to imagine any aspect of modern life existing without the wheel.

MATHEMATICS

When the Mesopotamians invented writing, they also created a way of recording numbers. Numbers were needed because writing was first used by farmers to keep an accurate record of the amount of grain that they grew or the number of cattle that they kept.

The Mesopotamians had two ways of counting. The first one was based on counting in units of sixty. This is called *sexagesimal* system of counting. We still use this way of counting today. When we measure time we count in sixties. There are sixty seconds in a minute and sixty minutes in an hour. In mathematics we still divide a circle into 360 parts called degrees: 360 is a multiple of 60 (6 x 60 = 360). Dividing the day into 12 daytime and 12 night-time hours is another Mesopotamian invention.

The other method of counting that the Mesopotamians used was based on what is called the *decimal* system. This method of counting was based on tens, hundreds and thousands. This *decimal* system is the one that we still use today.

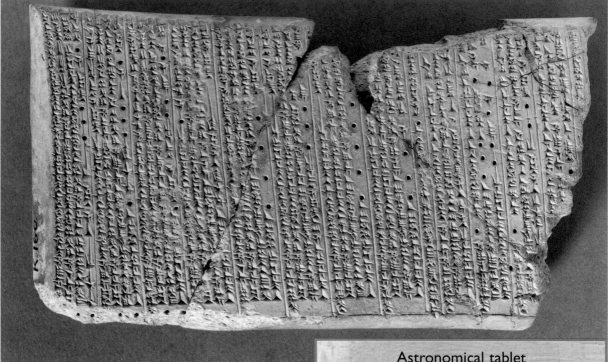

ASTRONOMY

Mesopotamian priests observed the night sky very carefully and made careful notes about the positions of planets and stars and the phases of the moon. They believed that the positions of the planets and stars could act as omens. In about 500 BCE the priests divided the night sky into twelve equal parts and grouped the stars in each of these parts into patterns called constellations. From these twelve divisions of the night sky the modern zodiac, the basis for star-signs and horoscopes, was developed.

MODERN MESOPOTAMIA

Mesopotamia is now modern-day Iraq. The Mesopotamian civilisation declined

WHAT DOES IT TELL US?

This astronomical tablet comes from the Royal Palace of Nineveh around 700 BCE. Along with written observations of events in the night sky it also charts the future movements of the stars and planets. This tells us that the priests were able to record what they saw in the sky and then believed they could work out what would happen in several months or years time.

with their defeat at the hands of the Persian king Cyrus the Great in 539 BCE. In 331 BCE, Alexander the Great, from Macedonia, conquered the entire region, officially ending the ancient Mesopotamian civilisation. The area was then conquered by the Arabs in 638 CE and the people converted to the Muslim faith. It was later controlled either by the Mongols or Turkey until the end of the First World War in 1918. After being briefly ruled by the British, Iraq achieved independence in 1921. There was a lot of unrest inside the country from the 1950s until the end of the 1970s when Saddam Hussein took power.

Since then Iraq has been involved in a war with Iran and invaded the neighbouring state of Kuwait. In 2003 a coalition army invaded Iraq and overthrew the government of Saddam Hussein. Despite the destruction of many of the country's ancient treasures, modern Iraqis continue to honour the contributions their Mesopotamian heritage has made to their culture and to the world – from the wheel to myths, to mathematics.

A modern Mesopotamian palace

WHAT DOES IT TELL US?
Saddam Hussein's palace was built in the 1980s. It is four stories high and is shaped like a ziggurat. It was built next to King Nebuchadnezzar's old palace. It shows us how much influence Mesopotamian civilisation still has on modern-day Iraq. Over the years, Iraqi leaders have wanted to show the people they ruled that they could be as strong as ancient Mesopotamian kings.

TIMELINE

4000 BCE First civilisations arise in Mesopotamia

3000 BCE Writing first developed in Mesopotamia

3000 BCE Wheels invented in Mesopotamia

2800 BCE First known ruler of the Sumerians, Etana, takes the throne

2335 BCE Sargon the Great becomes ruler of the Akkadians

2200 BCE Akkadian rule of Mesopotamia declines

2000 BCE Epic of Gilgamesh written down

2000 BCE Ziggarat at Ur built

1728 BCE Hammurabi becomes king of Babylon

1000 BCE Mesopotamians develop their own alphabet

630 BCE Nebuchadnezzar starts his reign over Babylon

539 BCE Persians conquer Mesopotamia

331 BCE Mesopotamia taken over by Alexander the Great

FIND OUT MORE

BOOKS

Peter Chrisp, *Mesopotamia*, Franklin Watts 2004

Stephanie Daley, *Myths from Mesopotamia*, Oxford University Press, 1998

John Malam, *Your Mesopotamia Homework Helper*, TickTock 2004

Julian Reade, *Mesopotamia*, British Museum Press, 2000

Michael Roaf, *Cultural Atlas of Mesopotamia and the Ancient Near East Facts on File*, 1990

WEBSITES

http://www.mesopotamia.co.uk/menu.html
An interactive site created by the British Museum exploring the main civilisations of Mesopotamia. It uses objects from the British Museum collections and has downloadable worksheets and online activities.

http://www.fordham.edu/halsall/ancient/asbook.html
This site contains texts from Mesopotamia. It includes the text of the Law Code of Hammurabi, the Epic of Gilgamesh and other Mesopotamian writings.

http://oi.uchicago.edu/OI/MUS/ED/TRC/MESO/mesohome.html
Educational materials on the Mesopotamians using the collections of the Oriental Institute of the University of Chicago.

http://www.crystalinks.com/meso.html
A good introduction to Mesopotamia with lots of images and a timeline.

GLOSSARY

Akkadia — Region of Mesopotamia in the south of modern-day Iraq.

Akkadians — The Akkadians lived around near what is modern-day Baghdad. Their main city was Agade which was founded by King Sargon in around 233 BCE.

Amelu — The Babylonian ruling class.

Ardu — The name for Babylonian slaves.

Assyria — Region of Mesopotamia in the north of modern-day Iraq.

Babylon — Region of Mesopotamia in the south of modern-day Iraq.

Carnelian — A stone that could be cut and polished and used in jewellery.

Chaldeans — The Chaldeans are sometimes called the Neo-Babylonians. They came from Southern Mesopotamia and ruled Babylonia from 612 BCE. The Chaldeans lost their empire to the Persians in 539 BCE.

Cuneiform — Style of writing used by the Mesopotamians. It was done by making marks in soft clay. The word cuneiform comes from the Latin word for 'wedge'.

Cylinder seal — A cylinder engraved with a design. The cylinder was rolled over soft clay which left an impression behind.

King List — A text recording the names of kings and the lengths of their reigns. The most famous king list comes from Sumer.

Lapis Lazuli — A deep blue semi-precious gemstone often used in Mesopotamian jewellery.

Law Codes — Texts recording various crimes and the penalties attached to them. The most famous code was the Law Code of Hammurabi.

Muskinu — Landless workers in Babylon.

Sumer — Region of Mesopotamia in the south of modern-day Iraq.

Talent — A unit of weight equal to 60 minas. It weighs about 30 kilograms.

Ziggurat — A pyramid-shaped structure with a temple built on the top.

INDEX

Akkadians 5, 6, 13
Alexander the Great 15
alphabets 33
An (god of heaven) 36
Anum 10
armies 13
armour 14, 15
Ashur 8, 36, 38
Assyrians 5-6, 9, 11, 13, 14, 38
astronomy 42, 44

Babylon 8, 9, 10, 18, 19, 36, 40
Babylonians 5, 6, 7, 9, 10-11, 13, 15, 32, 34
Bible, the 40, 42

Chaldeans 5
chariots 12, 13, 15, 21, 42
clay tablets 30, 32, 33, 35, 41
climate 4, 5, 30, 31
clothes 19-20
cuneiform 32, 33, 35, 41
cylinder seals 31, 35
Cyrus the Great, King 15, 45

demons 40-1
divorce 17

Enheduanna 18
Enki (god of water) 36
Enlil (god of air) 10, 36
Epic of Gilgamesh 38, 40, 42
Euphrates 4, 5, 6, 15, 29

farming 4, 5, 6, 7, 10, 27-31, 38
festivals 36, 38
floods 4, 6, 31
food 27, 28-9

games 26-7
glass 22
gods and goddesses 9, 18, 23, 36-41

Hammurabi, Code of 10-11, 17, 34, 35
Hammurabi, King 6, 7, 8, 10-11
Hanging Gardens of Babylon 18, 19
horses 12, 14, 15
houses 18
Hussein, Saddam 45

Iraq 7, 45
irrigation 5, 30-1

jewellery 20-1, 39

Ki (goddess of earth) 36
kings 8-10, 23, 41

Marduk 36
mathematics 42, 43
metalwork 21, 27
music 25-6

Naram-Sin, King 9
Nebuchadnezzar II, King 18, 19, 45
Nineveh 9, 24, 44
number systems 7, 43

palaces 18, 19
Persians 7, 13, 15, 45
pottery 23
priests and priestesses 17, 18, 20, 23, 37, 39, 44

Sargon the Great, King 13
Sennacherib, King 24
Shalmaneser III, King 11
Shamash, Sun God 10
slaves 11
soldiers 12, 13, 14-15, 24
Sumerians 5, 6-7, 8, 9, 12, 21, 25, 31, 32, 33, 36
Susa 12

temples 10, 17, 18, 25, 37-40
Tiglath-Pileser III, King 13
Tigris 4, 5, 6, 7, 15, 29
Tower of Babel 40, 42
toys 24, 25
transport 42-3

Ur 8, 12, 18, 21, 22, 25, 26-7, 31, 36, 39, 42, 43
Uruk 6, 12, 35, 39

warfare 6, 12-15
weapons 12, 13, 14-15, 21
weaving 16
weights 43
wheels 7, 42-3
women 16-18
Wooley, Sir Leonard 26, 39
worship 36, 37-40
writing 7, 31, 32-5

ziggurat 39-40, 45